INTERNATIONAL STARS AT WAR

INTERNATIONAL
STARS ★ at ★ WAR

James E. Wise, Jr., and Scott Baron

NAVAL INSTITUTE PRESS
Annapolis, Maryland

Naval Institute Press
291 Wood Road
Annapolis, MD 21402

Library of Congress Cataloging-in-Publication Data
Wise, James E., 1930–
    International stars at war / James E. Wise, Jr., and Scott Baron.
      p. cm.
    Includes bibliographical references and index.
    ISBN 1-55750-965-4 (alk. paper)
    1. Actors as soldiers. 2. Actors as sailors. I. Baron, Scott, 1954–
II. Title.
PN1998.2.W54 2002
792'.028'0922—dc21

2002016600

Printed in the United States of America on acid-free paper ∞
09 08 07 06 05 04 03 02 9 8 7 6 5 4 3 2

First printing

*For Jim's endearing friends Al and Becky Burkhalter; for Cpl.
Joseph Baron, who fought the war to
end all wars; and for Pvt. Eric Scott Baron, USAR, and
Heath J. Baron—a man could ask for better sons,
but he'd have a ways to travel to find them.*

Contents

Part 2: Others Who Served

Part 3: Entertainers

Appendixes

Preface

International Stars at War is the last volume of our "Stars" series, which chronicles the military experiences of movie actors and actresses. The idea for the initial volume came from a book, *When Hollywood Went to War,* in which I learned that the American movie actor Wayne Morris was a Navy air ace during World War II (he shot down seven Japanese planes and was awarded two Air Medals and three Distinguished Flying Crosses). In fact, he was the only American actor to gain such renown during any American war.

I began to wonder what other American movie stars had served in the U.S. military and what personal experiences they may have had while at sea or in the field of battle. This led to interviews and correspondence with ex-Navy men Paul Newman, Douglas Fairbanks, Jr., Eddie Albert, Ernest Borgnine, and Kirk Douglas, to name just a few, and resulted in the publication of *Stars in Blue* in 1997. A second volume followed in 1999, *Stars in the Corps,* which profiled the U.S. Marine Corps service of Tyrone Power, Robert Ryan, Lee Marvin, Steve McQueen, Brian Dennehy, and others. Our third volume, *Stars in Khaki,* published in 2000, included actors such as Audie Murphy (America's most decorated World War II soldier), Ronald Reagan, Clint Eastwood, Mickey Rooney, Charles Durning, Tony Bennett, Art Carney, Elvis Presley, and Burt Lancaster. While writing the *Khaki* book we were invited by one of the World War II veterans we profiled, James Arness ("Marshal Matt Dillon" of *Gunsmoke* fame), who was wounded at Anzio, to assist him in writing his autobiography. Jim had never forgotten that searing experience and wished to include it in his life's story. Working with a man who is so much bigger than life was an exciting and gratifying experience. Jim Arness is a throwback to the much hallowed "greatest generation." He is a kind, thoughtful man, true to his word and a born leader. He is loved by all who know him and have worked with him. Burt Reynolds, who also appeared in *Gunsmoke* and wrote the preface to Jim's book, said it best: "Old friend, like it or not you and that show are what the word icon really represents."

Taking on the rest of the movie world proved a bit more difficult because of the many nationalities involved. But through the marvel of technology and the Internet we were able to contact numerous people who were willing to assist us in this effort.

As we close out this series I must pay special thanks to my co-authors, Anne Collier Rehill, Paul Wilderson, and Scott Baron. Without their untiring research, writing, and editing support these books would not have been written. As we mentioned in the other volumes, we owe a great debt to Natalie Hall, research assistant extraordinaire, whose invaluable assistance and dedication helped enormously in making these books come to fruition. I can never thank her enough.

Perhaps no one will again write such a series of books, but for now the wartime sacrifices of these men and women have been recorded for future generations. As these veterans leave us, their deeds will not have been forgotten. As long as movies are made, they remain a special corps of thespians who served their countries with pride and devotion.

James E. Wise, Jr.

Acknowledgments

As with the other "Stars" volumes, many assisted us by collecting and contributing materials used in the writing of this book. With our sincere thanks to all, and our apologies to those who are not mentioned here, we would like to acknowledge some special people: Natalie Hall, Beverly Rogers, Barry Whatton, Jack Green, Ron Mandelbaum, Sir Alec Guinness, Roger Moore, Patrick Macnee, Christopher Lee, Brian Coleman, George Toy, Ward Garing, A. D. Lieber, Kevin Reem, Susan Reimer, Doug McKeown, Barbara J. DeGennaro, Richard Mangan, Anne Herridge, and Mary V. Yates.

★

PART 1

Movie Actors Who Served in the Military

★

Richard Attenborough

In 1982 the epic film *Gandhi,* the story of India's Hindu Nationalist leader and social reformer who used passive resistance and civil disobedience to free the country from British rule, was released and shown in American theaters. The movie was awarded eight Oscars, and among those receiving the coveted awards was Sir Richard Attenborough, who was voted Best Director.

Attenborough had wished to film the story of Mohandas Gandhi since the 1960s. He remarked after receiving the award, "This is what I wanted to do more than anything else I've been involved with . . . everything I've done was sort of training. I didn't want to direct per se, I wanted to make *Gandhi.*"

Richard Samuel Attenborough was born in Cambridge, England, on 29 August 1923; he grew up the eldest of three sons. His father, Freder-

(Photofest)

Attenborough and his wife Sheila on their wedding day, 1945. (Richard
Attenborough collection)

ick, a scholar and principal of the University College in Leicester, exposed
his sons to literature and music at an early age. Attenborough decided on
an acting career early on and performed in school and amateur productions while attending Wyggeston Grammar School. Upon completing his
formal education in 1940, he was awarded the Leverhulme Scholarship
to the Royal Academy of Dramatic Arts (RADA) in London.

While a student at RADA, Attenborough made his first professional
stage and screen appearances: on stage in 1941 at London's Palmer's
Green in Eugene O'Neill's play *Ah Wilderness,* and on screen in Noel
Coward's film *In Which We Serve* (1942).

While filming *In Which We Serve,* Coward introduced Attenborough to Lord Louis Mountbatten, on whose wartime experiences the book and movie were based. That friendship would be renewed almost forty-nine years later during the filming of *Gandhi.*

Perhaps inspired by his father, who was the local chairman of a committee assisting Jewish refugees from Germany, Attenborough enlisted in the Royal Air Force (RAF) in June 1943. In 1944, while assigned as an airman second class, he was taken out of pilot's training and transferred to the RAF film unit at Pinewood. He took a leading role in the morale-raising movie *Journey Together* (1945), with Edward G. Robinson. Upon completing the film, Attenborough requested assignment to an operational unit, and he finished the war flying air reconnaissance missions over Germany.

For the ten years following his demobilization in 1946, Attenborough worked as a stage actor. Dissatisfied with the quality of the roles he was offered in the 1950s, he formed his own production company, Beaver Films, with scriptwriter Bryan Forbes, and their first film, *The Angry Silence* (1960), was a critical success. A year later he founded Allied Filmmakers. When Attenborough was appointed chairman of RADA in 1970, he had appeared in fifty films and had won numerous awards, among them the British Academy of Film and Television Arts (BAFTA) Award for Best Actor for *Guns at Batasi* (1964) and *Séance on a Wet Afternoon* (1964). He also was honored with Golden Globe awards for Best Supporting Actor for *The Sand Pebbles* (1966) and *Doctor Dolittle* (1967). Other films that brought him acting accolades were *The Great Escape* (1963), *Flight of the Phoenix* (1966), and *Jurassic Park* (1992).

In addition to *Gandhi,* Attenborough went on to produce and/or direct a series of highly regarded films: *Oh! What a Lovely War* (1969), *Young Winston* (1971), *A Bridge Too Far* (1977), *A Chorus Line* (1985), *Cry Freedom* (1987), *Chaplin* (1992), *Shadowlands* (1993), and *In Love and War* (1996).

Attenborough was made a Commander of the Order of the British Empire and was knighted by Queen Elizabeth II in 1976. He was awarded the Jean Renoir Humanitarian Award in 1987 and became a baron in 1993.

Attenborough married actress Sheila Sim in 1945, and they have one son and two daughters. The couple currently reside in Surrey, England.

★

Jean-Pierre Aumont

French-born actor Jean-Pierre Aumont fought with the Free French forces in Italy and France and was awarded the Legion of Honor and the croix de guerre. During his eighteen months with the 1st Free French Division he kept a journal of his experiences, which he included in his autobiography, *Sun and Shadow,* published in 1977.

In October 1943 Aumont boarded a Liberty ship in England bound for Oran, Algeria. As his ship zigzagged through eastern Atlantic waters toward an uncertain future, the troops held midnight parties to alleviate the tension. In the pitch black of the night he befriended an English soldier who appeared but a shadow in the dark. They talked about France, its literature, and the theater; the "Brit" was articulate and appeared to know a great deal about French plays. As dawn broke Aumont found that his shipmate was Peter Ustinov.

(Photofest)

After a brief layover in Oran, Aumont departed for Algiers by train and upon his arrival was assigned to the 1st Free French Division, which made history at Bir-Hakeim and El Alamein giving the Allies their first complete desert victories. On 13 April 1944 his unit shipped out of Bizerte, Tunisia, for Naples, Italy, where upon their arrival they camped at Alba Nuova. A month later they were moved to the front lines, where Allied armies had been fighting for four months trying to penetrate the Gustav Line at Cassino. The Allied command finally decided that the only way to break the stalemate was to overpower the enemy. The Germans were outnumbered by more than three to one in artillery, armor, and aircraft. On 11 May the entire Allied front opened fire. The Gustav Line became a hellish battlefield, with the Allied forces finally prevailing. Polish troops were the first to take Monte Cassino. Although Aumont's unit was fighting just eight miles away, they did not find out about it until they heard the news on their radio.

Ten days later Gen. Charles de Gaulle arrived at the front to make a short speech and award individual medals. He left the unit with the words "All of you play an essential role in the great campaign of 1944 which is just beginning. Gentlemen, it is my profound honor to salute you." On 23 May, Aumont was detailed as a liaison officer to the U.S. 75th Tank Battalion. They were ordered to take the town of Pontecorvo, about twenty miles northwest of Cassino. Aumont manned his Sherman tank and together with infantrymen advanced to a point southwest of the town where his unit came under heavy enemy fire. A shot grazed his neck without wounding him. That night he slept under his tank next to the corpse of a Senegalese. Moving forward at dawn, they were met by a concentration of enemy antitank weapons and a German SS regiment. Two of his unit's tank destroyers were hit and set ablaze. They were subsequently forced to stop at the side of Mount Leucio. Wounded enemy prisoners were brought back through their lines; many of the German soldiers were in their teens. Aumont and his men reconnoitered Mount Leucio and continued to encounter heavy enemy fire.

The link-up between the Americans who had landed at Anzio and the bulk of the Fifth Army that was at Cassino took place as Aumont's unit reached Pontecorvo only to find that the town had been taken by French Marines and Polish forces.

During World War II, international film star Jean-Pierre Aumont fought with the Free French forces in Italy and France, and for his service he received the Legion of Honor and the Croix de Guerre. (Photofest)

On 4 June 1944, Rome was liberated, and the 1st Free French Division paraded down Piazza Venezia and along the Corso del Impero. They were met by crowds of people delirious with enthusiasm, throwing flowers at the marching troops and offering them wine.

On 10 June the Allied soldiers were on the front lines again in an attempt to liberate Siena, situated in north central Italy about ninety miles southeast of the port city of Livorno. Numerous French soldiers and their commanders were killed by land mines, which now became a deadly hazard to their advance. Smith, an American lieutenant who was commanding the tank "Pin-up Girl," was wounded, so Aumont filled in for him. After advancing a few more miles, a barrage of German shells began to explode around them. A German patrol was sighted ahead of them; Aumont fired the machine gun mounted on his tank, and several of the Germans were hit and fell to the ground. With this, the others raised their hands and surrendered. On 23 July the Italian campaign was finished for the French divisions. They had suffered seven hundred dead and two thousand wounded during the fighting. The divisions were withdrawn from battle, transported to Naples, and loaded into LSTs (landing ships, tank). All wondered about their destination. Would it be Yugoslavia or southern France?

Aumont was sent as a liaison officer to the U.S. 3d Infantry Division, where he learned that the Free French divisions were to be part of an invasion of southern France. As the LSTs and support combatants began their journey for the shores of France, a launch came bounding through the formation. Standing on the foredeck of the vessel was a bareheaded man wearing civilian clothes and flashing the famous "V for victory" sign; it was Winston Churchill. It was arranged that Aumont would be disembarked with the first elements of the Free French forces. He waded ashore at Cavalaire as naval ships and Allied bombers bombarded the area. His job was to contact as many members of the local resistance as possible. On the way to the U.S. 3d Division headquarters he passed a young woman, her husband, and their little boy. "Did you expect the landing?" he asked. The French family answered that bombs had been dropping on their heads for eight days, and one would have had to be a simpleton not to expect it.

On 23 August 1944, Paris was liberated. However, Toulon and Marseille were still occupied, and Aumont was wounded by eighty-eight pieces of shrapnel in his legs. After being hospitalized for a month, he was able to rejoin his division at Lyon. On 13 September, Aumont was promoted to first lieutenant, awarded the Legion of Honor, and chosen to serve as aide-de-camp to General Brosset, commander of the 1st Free French Division. General Brosset was a dynamic leader, respected and loved by his men. One day Aumont was with General Brosset in a jeep that the general was driving (as always) at breakneck speed, hoping to make Giromagny by evening. As they approached a bridge at seventy miles an hour, the general braked, and the jeep skidded and flipped into the water. They both went down with the jeep into the fast-running river. Aumont just managed to free himself and reach the surface, but the general drowned.

Aumont was given a month to convalesce. His wrist was in a cast, and the wounds in his knees had reopened. He was asked by his friend, the noted actor Claude Dauphin, to act in a play that would benefit the Free French military. He returned to the front at Alsace in January 1945 after giving fifteen performances. Although his division had been sent to rest and his relief had arrived, he was saddened that he would not be participating in the final assault on Germany. However, he briefly rejoined his division and did get to see the Rhine. He then departed for home and his discharge.

A charming, durable leading man of French, American, and international films, Aumont was born on 5 January 1909 in Paris. He made his stage debut in 1930 and appeared in his first film in 1931. He became an established star after appearing in Jean Cocteau's play *La machine infernale* (The Infernal Machine, 1934).

Following World War II he returned to his theatrical career and performed in numerous international films. Always popular with American audiences, he visited the United States frequently to appear in stage plays, television shows, and movies. He was married four times, to French film actress Blanche Montel; Hollywood siren Maria Montez, who died during their marriage; and film actress Marisa Pavan, whom he married, divorced, and remarried. In all, Aumont appeared in seventy-four films, including *The Cross of Lorraine* (1943), *Lili* (1959), *The Devil at Four O'Clock* (1961), *Castle Keep* (1969), and *Day for Night* (1973). His last American-made film was *Jefferson in Paris* (1995). He died at the age of ninety-two at his home in Saint-Tropez on the French Riviera.

★

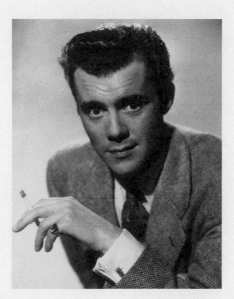

Dirk Bogarde

D irk Bogarde was born Derek Jules Gaspard Ulric Niven Van den Bogarde in the Hampstead borough of London on 28 March 1921. His half-Dutch father was the art editor of the *London Times,* and his mother was the daughter of Forrest Niven, a popular actor and painter. Young Bogarde showed an inclination for art, entering the Chelsea School of Art in London at age twelve and winning a scholarship to the Royal College of Art when he was sixteen.

Interested in the theater from his youth, Bogarde found his first job as a set-maker's assistant at the "Q" Theatre in London. He made his stage debut in 1939 and was working in the theater at the beginning of World War II.

Bogarde enlisted in the British Army's Royal Corps of Signals in

Bogarde with Alec Guinness in *Damn the Defiant!* (1962). (Photofest)

1941 and was sent to Officer Cadets Battle School early in 1942. He was commissioned a full lieutenant and a liaison officer with the infantry. He was assigned to a photographic interpretation unit of Army intelligence, with which he saw service in both Europe and the Far East. One account has him landing at Normandy on D-Day, and two of his sketches of the invasion were later purchased by the British Imperial War Museum. He carried his sketchbook throughout the European campaign and was present at the battle for the Arnhem bridge in September 1944. He was among the troops that liberated the Bergen-Belsen concentration camp, then was transferred to the Pacific in time to participate in Operation Zipper in Burma. He finished the war with the rank of major and was discharged in 1946 after returning from Singapore aboard the *Monarch of Burma*.

Bogarde began acting in the theater in 1947. The experience led to a contract with the J. Arthur Rank Organization that resulted in his appearing in thirty films over a fourteen-year period. In all, Bogarde has made over sixty films, including *A Tale of Two Cities* (1958), *The Servant* (1963), *Justine* (1969), and *The Night Porter* (1974). He began to write in the late 1970s and has published autobiographies as well as novels.

Charles Boyer

His screen lovers included some of the most beautiful women in the world. Marlene Dietrich, Olivia de Havilland, Ingrid Bergman, Greta Garbo, Bette Davis, Joan Fontaine, and Claudette Colbert all surrendered to his Gallic charm, rich voice, and classic good looks.

In real life Charles Boyer's heart belonged solely to his wife of forty-four years, British-born Patricia (Pat) Paterson, whom he met and married in 1934, when she was a Fox Studios starlet. So deep and abiding was their love that on 26 August 1978, two days after his wife's death from cancer, he ended his own life with an overdose of barbiturates rather than carry on alone.

Charles Boyer was born in Figeac, a village in southwestern France, on 28 August 1899. His father, Maurice, was a prosperous dealer in farm

(Photofest)

machinery, and his mother, Louise, an amateur musician. Blessed with a remarkable memory, he is said to have been able to recite entire poems at the age of three, and by the age of eight he was writing and performing plays and skits with his playmates in a granary on the Boyer farm.

When Boyer was ten years old, his father died of a stroke, and his mother sold the family business to devote her time to raising her son. By the age of eleven, Boyer was in love with acting and the theater, encouraged by stolen afternoons at the cinema and visits to Paris with his mother to take in plays and concerts. Although Mme. Boyer tolerated his infatuation with the stage, her intention was that young Charles would grow up to become a lawyer or perhaps a priest.

When World War I broke out in 1914, Boyer volunteered as an orderly at a nearby hospital. He rotated his more mundane duties with entertaining convalescing soldiers and staff with impromptu revue sketches, using young nurses and others as part of the cast. But it was an encounter with a visiting film company toward the end of the war that changed his life. The company was in a nearby village shooting exterior footage on location for the film *Travail*. Boyer became friends with one of the players, who obtained a bit part for him, and convinced his mother that he had a brilliant future in acting.

Mme. Boyer finally gave in and consented to Charles's following the theater, insisting, however, that he first complete his education. After graduating from the local lyceum in 1918, Boyer left for Paris and enrolled at the Sorbonne, where he pursued (and eventually attained) a degree in philosophy while at the same time seeking roles on the Paris stage.

In the heady postwar atmosphere of Paris, Boyer made the acquaintance of numerous actors and others in the theater, and was accepted at the Conservatoire national supérior de musique et de déclamation, an advanced professional program for actors and artists. He began taking classes and studying his craft in earnest.

In 1920 the leading man in the play *Les jardins de Murcie* (The Gardens of Murcia) fell ill, and its director, hearing of Boyer's remarkable memory, approached the young actor to ask if he could learn the role in the twelve hours before the play was due to open. He did, becoming an overnight sensation in the role. Additional roles followed, as did lucrative offers to appear and act in a new medium, film. By the mid-1920s, Boyer was one of the busiest actors in France, and one of

Boyer in *Gaslight* (1944). During World War I, Boyer served as a hospital orderly. Boyer was already an established film star in 1939, when war broke out between Germany and France. He enlisted in the French army, nevertheless, and—at the age of forty—was assigned to the 37th Artillery. It wasn't long, however, before Private Boyer was mustered out of his regiment to serve in Hollywood as a goodwill ambassador for the Allied cause. (Photofest)

the best known, both as a romantic lead on the Paris stage and for his work in silent film.

Boyer first came to Hollywood in 1929, and although he spoke French, Spanish, Italian, and German, he was limited by his lack of English, which he began to study immediately. MGM's Irving Thalberg took an interest in Boyer, casting him in French versions of MGM films for the European market, and Boyer stayed busy on both sides of the Atlantic.

Although a popular actor in his French homeland, Boyer was initially dissatisfied with his progress in American film and twice returned to France in frustration. He credits his success to producer Walter Wanger, who persuaded him to appear with his countrywoman

Claudette Colbert in the film *Private Worlds* (1935). Boyer's American career took off as the women of America fell in love with the suave Frenchman, captivated by his accent, his voice, and "those eyes."

It was during this period that Boyer attended a dinner party where he met a young English actress, Pat Paterson, on contract to Fox Studios. It was love at first sight. They were engaged within weeks and married within months. Even his close friend Maurice Chevalier was surprised, observing that Boyer could have had his pick of women.

His film career continued to thrive, with leading roles in *Shanghai* (1935); *The Garden of Allah* (1936), with Marlene Dietrich; *Conquest* (1937), in which he played Napoleon to Greta Garbo's Josephine; and *Algiers* (1938), in which he is erroneously reported to have murmured to Hedy Lamarr, "Come with me to the Casbah."

Boyer recognized early the threat posed by Hitler and Nazi Germany, and he spoke out against fascism. He was in Nice, France, for a visit in 1939 when war broke out between Germany and France. Boyer promptly enlisted in the French Army at the age of forty.

Assigned to the 37th Artillery, Private Boyer remained in uniform only a short time before being mustered out of his regiment to return to Hollywood. Those in authority reasoned that he could make a greater contribution to the war effort as a goodwill ambassador than as just another private second class working a switchboard behind the lines. He continued to support Gen. Charles de Gaulle after Germany occupied Paris in June 1940, and he actively supported the French resistance.

During World War II, in addition to making films, he served as president of the Hollywood Committee for French War Relief and made appearances speaking out against the Vichy government in France. In 1943 he was awarded an honorary Academy Award for his "progressive cultural achievement" in establishing the French Research Foundation in Los Angeles, which worked to promote positive Franco-American relations. During the filming of *Gaslight* (1944), his wife, Pat, gave birth to their only child, Michael Boyer, of whom he was so proud that co-star Ingrid Bergman remarked, "You'd think no one in the world had ever had a son before."

Following the war, Boyer continued to appear in films, as well as on the stage, but with an eye more on character roles, perhaps sensing that his time as a romantic lead was drawing to a close. He also sought success in an emerging medium, television. With actors David Niven and Dick Powell he formed a television production company, Four Star Productions, in 1951. (The original "fourth star," Joel McCrea, backed out and was replaced by actress Ida Lupino.) Together they produced a series, *Four Star Theatre,* which lasted six seasons, with the actors rotating as leads in the show's half-hour comedies and dramas.

Boyer's film work continued into the 1960s and early 1970s. He appeared with Leslie Caron and Maurice Chevalier in *Fanny* (1961), with Audrey Hepburn and Peter O'Toole in *How to Steal a Million* (1966), and with Robert Redford and Jane Fonda in *Barefoot in the Park* (1967). Younger audiences remember him as the High Lama in the 1973 remake of the film *Lost Horizon,* whose international cast included Peter Finch, Liv Ullmann, John Gielgud, Michael York, and Sally Kellerman.

Although nominated four times for a Best Actor Oscar—for *Conquest* (1937), *Algiers* (1938), *Gaslight* (1944), and *Fanny* (1961)—his only award from the Academy was the honorary award in 1943.

Boyer's final years were marked by tragedy. His son, despondent over a failed romance, committed suicide in 1965. In 1977 his beloved Pat was diagnosed with cancer, and he devoted himself to caring for her during her illness. She succumbed to the disease on 24 August 1978. After putting his affairs in order, he took an overdose of barbiturates and joined his wife in death two days later. He is buried beside her at Holy Cross cemetery in Culver City, just outside Los Angeles.

Richard Burton

Laurence Olivier is said to have remarked that Richard Burton squandered his talent to become a household name rather than the great Shakespearean actor he seemed destined to become. Certainly the turbulent life Burton led throughout his career subsumed his vast talent. With his resonant voice, articulate delivery, and commanding presence on stage or on screen, he captivated his audiences like few other actors of his day.

Richard Walter Jenkins, Jr., was born in Pontrhydyfen, Wales, on 10 November 1925, the twelfth of thirteen children of a coal miner father. His mother died during the delivery of the thirteenth child, and young Jenkins was raised from the age of two by his eldest sister. Encouraged by his schoolmaster, Philip Burton, he turned to acting. Burton's tutelage developed Jenkins's remarkable voice and smoothed out the traces of his rough upbringing. He eventually became Philip Burton's ward and assumed the schoolmaster's last name.

Richard Burton first performed on stage at the age of fifteen, appearing in a local production of Bernard Shaw's *The Apple Cart*. In 1943, shortly after turning eighteen, he entered Exeter College at Oxford and at the same time enlisted as an air cadet in the Royal Air Force (RAF) Air Training Corps 499, H Squadron, at Port Talbot. He took basic training two days a week while attending classes. After six months at Oxford, Burton was sent to Torquay Air Base for his RAF classification examinations. He hoped to be trained as a pilot, but an eyesight deficiency resulted in his being classified as a navigator trainee.

By 1944, the Allies controlled the skies over Europe, and there was a decreasing need for aircrews. In May 1945, after finishing basic training in navigation, Burton was en route by ship to Winnipeg, Canada, for advanced navigational training when Germany surrendered. He was still in training when Japan capitulated three months later. After completing his training, he was ordered back to England to await demobilization.

Burton had to wait more than two years to be demobilized—combat veterans were given priority—and he spent the time stationed at a succession of RAF bases across England. He played for a while on a base rugby team and was working as a clerk in an RAF hospital in Wiltshire when his demobilization orders arrived. He was discharged as an aircraftsman first class on 16 December 1947.

While enrolled in the RAF short course program in April 1944, Burton had performed in a production of Shakespeare's *Measure for Measure*. After the performance he was approached by Hugh Beaumont, a prominent London producer, who was impressed with the young man's talent. He told Burton that if he was serious about becoming an actor, he should look him up after the war. Upon his discharge, Burton declined returning to Oxford and headed for the London stage and Hugh Beaumont. True to his word, Beaumont saw to it that Burton got an acting contract at £500 a year. Burton was exultant; it was more money than any of his family had ever made in their lives.

Burton appeared in his first film, *The Last Days of Dolwyn,* in 1948. Though he was cast in several movies over the next few years, he spent most of his time performing Shakespeare on stage with the

Burton with actress Sandy Dennis in *Who's Afraid of Virginia Woolf?*
(1966). He was training as an RAF navigator in Canada when Germany surrendered in 1945. (Photofest)

Old Vic Company in London. In 1952 he traveled to Hollywood for
the first time, appearing opposite Olivia de Havilland in *My Cousin
Rachel* (1952), for which he was nominated for an Oscar for Best Supporting Actor. He followed with *The Robe* in 1953, this time getting
an Oscar nomination for Best Actor. Five more Best Actor nominations would follow: *Becket* (1964); *The Spy Who Came in from the
Cold* (1965); *Who's Afraid of Virginia Woolf?* (1966), in which he co-
starred with his wife, Elizabeth Taylor, who won a Best Actress Oscar
for her performance; *Anne of the Thousand Days* (1969); and *Equus*
(1977). During his film career Burton performed in fifty-five movies.
His other notable film appearances included *Cleopatra* (1963), Shakespeare's *The Taming of the Shrew* (1967), and several war movies: *The
Desert Rats* (1953), *Bitter Victory* (1958), *The Longest Day* (1962),
Where Eagles Dare (1969), *Raid on Rommel* (1971), and *The Wild
Geese* (1978). Burton also continued to appear in numerous stage productions such as *Camelot* (1960; American tour in 1980–81), *Hamlet* (1964), *Equus* (1976), and *Private Lives* (1983).

His first marriage, in 1949, to Welsh actress Sybil Williams produced two daughters and ended in divorce as a result of his much publicized offscreen romance with Elizabeth Taylor, whom he had met when they co-starred in *Cleopatra*. Burton twice married and divorced Taylor (1964–74 and 1975–76). His third marriage, to Susan Hunt, also ended in divorce, and his last marriage was to Sally Hay in 1983.

Richard Burton died of a stroke on 5 August 1984, in Geneva, Switzerland, where he had taken up residence. He was buried there wearing red, the national color of Wales.

★

Michael Caine

British actor Michael Caine was working as a file clerk at Peak Films when he was called up for national service and drafted into the British Army in May 1951, during the Korean War. Private Micklewhite (his born name), Fusilier #22486547, remembered his service with less than fondness, especially the killing. He was sent for occupation duty on the Rhine, in the town of Iserlohn near Dortmund. Germany's Field Marshal Erwin Rommel was buried there, and Caine recalled numerous fistfights with Afrika Korps veterans. He never volunteered, and his "low profile" was so low that his sergeant put him in the front rank so that he could keep track of him.

Caine was offered the choice between extending his tour of duty one year or being sent to Korea. So on 28 April 1952, Private Micklewhite, 9th Platoon, C Company, 1st Battalion Royal Fusiliers,

(Photofest)

Caine with actress Camilla Sparv at the premiere of *Murderer's Row* (1967). As a member of the 1st Royal Battalion Royal Fusiliers, he saw combat in the Korean War. (Photofest)

Queen's Royal Regiment, was sent to Warley Barracks, Brentwood, Essex, in preparation for overseas shipment to Korea. On 26 June he sailed from Liverpool, via Ceylon, to Korea, arriving on 4 August.

On 26 August his unit relieved the King's Shropshire Light Infantry at the Sami Chon River, opposite Chinese troops. He remembered mass attacks by the Chinese in which only one in four soldiers had rifles and they would retrieve weapons from fallen comrades as the attacks moved forward. Despite the extensive combat, what Caine recalled most vividly were the rats; they seemed to be everywhere. He turned down a promotion to lance corporal so that he could leave the Army the way he had entered, as a private. Caine contracted malaria while in Korea and continued to suffer the effects of the disease long after his discharge in 1953.

Born Maurice Joseph Micklewhite on Old King's Road in London on 14 March 1933, Caine grew up in humble circumstances in the Southwark section of the city. At the start of World War II his father, Maurice, Sr., went into the Army and was with the British Expeditionary Force trapped on the beaches of Dunkirk. He later served with the Eighth Army in Sicily and Italy.

Caine became separated from his family during a German bombardment of London. Placed in a foster home, he was not reunited with his family for a year. They spent the rest of the war living with twelve other homeless families on a farm outside Norfolk.

Returning to a destroyed flat in London after the war, Caine enrolled in a Jewish parochial school, not because he was Jewish but because it was the only school available. His parents hoped he would become a Queen's Guard or a London policeman, but he wanted to be an actor. He left school at sixteen and worked at a variety of jobs such as dishwasher, clerk, and office boy before his call-up.

After leaving the Army, Caine returned to London, where he studied acting while working in a butter factory and, later, a meat market. His start in the theater was as an assistant stage manager at the Westminster Repertory Theatre in Sussex. He changed his name to Michael Caine, a choice inspired by a marquee advertising the film *The Caine Mutiny* (1954). During the late 1950s he played bit parts in provincial theaters, appeared frequently on British television, and began to be cast in small roles in feature films.

His breakaway role as the arrogant British officer in *Zulu* (1964) brought him critical acclaim. Better parts followed, in *The Ipcress File* (1965), *Alfie* (1966), *Too Late the Hero* (1969), and *The Man Who Would Be King* (1975). Caine won a British Academy of Film and Television Arts (BAFTA) Award for Best Actor for *Educating Rita*

(1983) and an Oscar as Best Supporting Actor for *Hannah and Her Sisters* (1986). He won a second Best Supporting Actor Oscar for *The Cider House Rules* (1999). Other recent films include *Little Voice* (1989), *Quills* (2000), and *Last Orders* (2001).

Caine published an autobiography, *What's It All About,* in 1992. Fans of this gifted star will recognize the phrase as coming from the famous title song of the movie *Alfie.*

Maurice Chevalier

Born in a working-class section of Paris on 12 September 1888, Maurice Chevalier was the youngest of nine children of a house painter father who deserted the family when Chevalier was eight years old. His mother became ill and was hospitalized, and the children were sent to orphanages.

In the orphanage, Chevalier was apprenticed as an engraver and later as an electrician, but he was destined for the stage, and he made his singing debut at age twelve. Before his mother became ill, he had helped support the family by singing in cafes and music halls, where he enjoyed moderate success. He was already a popular entertainer and had appeared in French silent films when he was drafted into the French Army on 1 December 1913. (He had been postponing his compulsory service since 1908.)

(Photofest)

With war looming in Europe, Chevalier was assigned to the French 35th Infantry Regiment in garrison at Belfort, where he occasionally performed for his fellow soldiers. After the declaration of war in August 1914, his unit was transferred to Melun, outside Paris. At the Battle of Cutry, his unit was ordered to advance under heavy enemy fire. Private Second Class Chevalier was wounded and taken prisoner in his first action. Wounded in the lung, he awoke in a German hospital.

Chevalier was interned in a German POW camp at Altengrabow, where he volunteered as a medical orderly. He remained a prisoner for twenty-six months until his release through a prisoner exchange. While he was interned he entertained the prisoners by putting on shows. He also took English lessons from a British prisoner, Sgt. Ronald Kennedy, knowing that he would need English to extend his career beyond France.

After the war Chevalier resumed his French film career. In the late 1920s he went to America and made pictures for Paramount, United Artists, and MGM, earning a reported $20,000 a week. Films like *Innocents in Paris* (1929), *Love Me Tonight* (1932), and *The Merry Widow* (1934) increased his popularity with American audiences.

Chevalier returned to Europe in the late 1930s and was dining with the duke and duchess of Windsor when the Nazis declared war and invaded Poland on 1 September 1939. He chose to remain in France rather than withdraw to England or the United States. He sang at gun emplacements, in mess halls, and along the Maginot Line, often with Josephine Baker.

Chevalier remained in Vichy France for the duration of the war. He occasionally sang on German-controlled radio and remained relatively unmolested by the Germans because of his popularity. For this reason it was rumored that he was collaborating with the Germans. There were even reports of his being shot as a collaborator by the Maquis (the French resistance) after the war; the story appeared in the *Washington Post*. However, an investigation by American military authorities disclosed that he had spent the majority of the occupation quietly at his home near Cannes. Josephine Baker and others spoke out on his behalf, and he was eventually cleared by the French government.

Chevalier did agree to do one concert in Germany during the war— ironically, at Altengrabow, the same camp where he had been interned during World War I. The Germans made the most of the propaganda opportunity and implied that he was performing to support the Axis cause. But in fact he had agreed to do it only on the condition that ten prisoners from his home town would be released. It is also possible that he cooperated because of threats to his half-Jewish nineteen-year-old mistress, Nina, and her family. The Germans were deporting foreign-born Jews and may have used this as leverage.

After the war Chevalier entertained Allied troops throughout Europe and was awarded the croix de guerre and the Legion of Merit, though rumors of his collaboration dogged him for the rest of his life. He was awarded a special Oscar in 1958, and he died in France in 1972.

★

M. E. Clifton-James

I n his entire film career, he appeared in only two films. The greatest performance of his life was neither captured on film nor performed on stage but resulted in the saving of countless lives during the Allied invasion of Normandy on 6 June 1944.

M. E. Clifton-James was born in Perth, Australia, in 1898 (some accounts say 1897), and he fought with the British Army during World War I in the trenches of France, where he was seriously gassed. After the war Clifton-James took to the stage, and he was working on the London stage at the start of World War II. He once again enlisted in the Army and was serving as a lieutenant in the Royal Army Pay Corps in 1944 when he received a telephone call from Lt. Col. David Niven inviting him to a meeting to discuss a proposed film project. Niven, a former film star, was then assigned to the Kinematograph (film) sec-

(Photofest)

tion of the British Army, having earlier served in the infantry and commandos.

The two agreed to meet, but at the meeting, Niven introduced Clifton-James to an agent of MI5 (British Military Intelligence) and left the room. The call, and the proposed film, had been a ruse to arrange this meeting. Clifton-James bore an extraordinarily close physical resemblance to Gen. (later Field Marshal) Bernard Montgomery, the victorious commander at El Alamein, and MI5 hoped to use Clifton-James to impersonate him for an upcoming operation.

The objective of the mission, Operation Copperhead (also referred to as Operation Hambone), was to deceive the Germans into believing that the anticipated Allied invasion of Europe would occur in southern France. The plan was for Clifton-James to impersonate Monty and travel first to Gibraltar and later Algiers, in North Africa, where his appearance, certain to be noticed by Axis agents, would add credibility to the idea that the invasion would come from the south. There were rumors that Clifton-James almost blew his cover by smoking cigars and drinking (Monty did neither), but the impersonation must have been successful, for the Germans were taken unaware on 6 June.

Clifton-James returned to the Pay Corps following the assignment. He returned to civilian life and acting after the war ended. He wrote a book about his wartime experiences, *The Counterfeit General,* which was made into the film *I Was Monty's Double* (1958), in which he played both himself and General Montgomery. He also appeared in the film *Blanche Fury* (1947), playing a prison warden, but otherwise he seems to have returned to obscurity. He is featured on a postage stamp from Guyana, commemorating World War II film stars. He died in Worthing, Sussex, England, on 8 May 1963.

Ronald Colman

Probably one of Ronald Colman's most memorable film roles was that of Robert Gordon in *Lost Horizon,* a fictional tale about a group of British subjects fleeing Baskul, China, by plane to escape an unruly local Chinese government. Instead of being flown to safety, the plane—piloted by a mysterious oriental—flies into the mountains of Tibet and eventually runs out of fuel and crashes. The passengers, led by Gordon, escape injury and are rescued by monks and taken to a land of mystery hidden in the mountains, a paradise where people live in complete happiness and never age. Gordon was brought there for a specific purpose, which is explained to him during his conversations with the High Lama.

The haunting story was cast perfectly with Jane Wyatt, John Howard, Edward Everett Horton, Margo, Thomas Mitchell, and Sam

(Photofest)

Colman with actor Sam Jaffe in *Lost Horizon* (1937). A soldier in the London Scotts Regiment, Colman was among the first troops sent to France, and he fought in the first battle of Ypres (October–November 1914). (Photofest)

Jaffe (as the High Lama). The book itself became so popular that it was the first ever to be published in paperback.

The classic suave and romantic film hero, Ronald Charles Colman was born in Richmond, Surrey, England, on 9 February 1891, the son of Charles and Marjory (Fraser) Colman. His father was a silk importer. He attended Hadley School in preparation for his eventual enrollment at Oxford. Though he appeared in theatrical productions at Hadley, his mind was set on becoming an engineer.

His father died when Colman was only sixteen, and further study was out of the question since young Colman had to work to help support the family. He took a job as an office boy at a London steamship company and worked there for five years while continuing to appear in amateur theatricals as a member of Bancroft's Dramatic Society.

In 1909, Colman joined the 14th London Scots Regiment and

served a four-year hitch before leaving the regiment in 1913. He rejoined the regiment at Buckingham Gate on 5 August 1914, shortly after the start of World War I. The 14th London Scots Regiment was the first territorial unit to serve overseas with the regular Army. They were among the first troops sent to France, despite being relatively untrained. They were known as "the Ladies from Hell" because their uniforms included kilts.

Although scheduled for six months of training, the battalion was ordered overseas in September and set out from Southampton aboard the cattle ship *Winifredia*. The unit was sent to Villeneuve-Saint-Georges (about five miles north of Paris), where they were put to work loading ammunition and digging trenches. At the end of October 1914 the regiment was sent forward to Saint-Omer, transported in buses, and Colman fought in the first Battle of Ypres (October–November 1914). He was later wounded at Messines, by shrapnel from an exploding shell. He crawled backwards to his lines, facing the enemy, because he feared being found dead with his back to the enemy.

A cast was applied at a field hospital, and Colman was evacuated to England for further medical treatment. He worked desk jobs at a hospital awaiting a discharge, and he was invalided out of the Army on 6 May 1915, with an honorable discharge, a Mons Medal for distinguished service, and a limp. In 1916, shortly after his discharge, he made his debut on the London stage.

Colman performed in a series of small parts until the depression prompted him to try the New York stage in 1920. He got his first film part in 1922, when director Henry King cast him in *The White Sister,* which was filmed in Italy with famed actress Lillian Gish. His performance attracted the attention of Samuel Goldwyn, who offered him a contract, which Colman immediately accepted. Colman's first big film break came when he was cast in the Foreign Legion movie production *Beau Geste* (1926).

Colman went on to perform in over fifty films, including *A Tale of Two Cities* (1935), *The Prisoner of Zenda* (1937), and *If I Were King* (1938). He was nominated for an Oscar three times—for *Bulldog Drummond* and *Condemned* (both 1929) and for *Random Harvest* (1942)—before winning the Academy Award for Best Actor for *A Double Life* (1947).

Colman married twice during his lifetime. He divorced his first wife, Thelma Victoria Maud, in 1935. They had married in 1918 and for ten of those years they were separated. He married British actress Benita Hume in 1938, and they remained together until he died of pneumonia in Santa Barbara, California, in May 1958.

Sean Connery

Thomas Shane Connery was born in Edinburgh, Scotland, on 25 August 1930. He grew up during the depression and was delivering milk by the age of twelve. Located on his route was Fettes College, the alma mater of James Bond. He dropped out of school at fifteen and took a series of unskilled jobs including usher, truck driver, and coffin polisher.

In 1947, at the age of seventeen, Connery, a former sea cadet, enlisted in the Royal Navy for a twelve-year hitch (seven active, five reserve), hoping for glamour and girls. Shortly after he entered service at HMS *Lochinvar*, South Queensbury, he realized that he had made a mistake. He was trained at the gunnery school at Butlaw Camp, Rosyth, Scotland, and after a brief tour of duty with an antiaircraft unit, he was assigned as an able seaman aboard HMS *Formidable*, a

(Photofest)

The most famous 007 in the James Bond series, shown here in *From Russia with Love,* Connery enlisted in the Royal Navy at the age of seventeen and served at the shore base HMS *Formidable* just after World War II. (Photofest)

shore base in Portsmouth. He also boxed on Navy boxing teams and was twice tattooed: "Mum and Dad" and "Scotland Forever." Connery has stated that he did not adjust well to Navy discipline, and he was discharged with a duodenal ulcer after less than three years' service and given a disability pension.

After leaving the Navy, Connery considered a career as a soccer player but took a part in the chorus of a touring production of *South Pacific,* where he remained for eighteen months. He placed third in the Mr. Universe competition of 1953 and took a bit part in his first film, *Let's Make Up,* in 1955. He continued to appear in films ranging from *Darby O'Gill and the Little People* (1959) to *The Longest Day* (1962), but his real break came when he was cast in *Dr. No* (1962). Beating out competition like Cary Grant, Rex Harrison, Trevor Howard, Roger Moore, and Patrick McGoohan, Connery was selected to play James Bond, Ian Fleming's legendary secret agent. Six other Bond films followed for Connery: *From Russia with Love* (1963), *Goldfinger* (1964), *Thunderball* (1965), *You Only Live Twice* (1967), *Diamonds Are Forever* (1971), and *Never Say Never Again* (1983).

Connery's versatility as an actor has allowed him to play roles as varied as an Arab prince (*The Wind and the Lion,* 1975), a marshal in outer space (*Outland,* 1981), a Russian submarine commander (*The Hunt for Red October,* 1990), and a reclusive Pulitzer Prize–winning writer (2000). He won the Best Supporting Actor Oscar for his performance as the Irish cop Malone in *The Untouchables* (1987).

Voted *People Magazine*'s "Sexiest Man Alive" in 1989, Connery continues to make films and campaign for Scottish home rule.

★

Alain Delon

Since the late eighteenth century, France had controlled the areas of Vietnam, Laos, and Cambodia known collectively as the French colony of Indochina. During World War II, Indochina had been occupied by Japanese forces. Following Japan's defeat, France attempted to reestablish control.

These actions were opposed by the Viet Minh (League for the Independence of Vietnam, formed in 1941), and by its leader, Ho Chi Minh, who on 2 September 1945 proclaimed Vietnamese independence from France, establishing the Government of the Democratic Republic of Vietnam in Hanoi. The French government responded by sending troops, and a nine-year struggle ensued, culminating in the fall of the French stronghold at Dien Bien Phu in the western Tonkin province near the Laotian border.

(Photofest)

After the fifty-five-day siege, the surrounded French Expeditionary Force surrendered on 7 May 1954, forcing France to seek a political settlement. The battle had cost the French 2,293 killed, 5,134 wounded, and 10,000 captured. Viet Minh losses were 8,000 killed and 15,000 wounded. Among the notables at Dien Bien Phu at that time were American female war correspondent Marguerite Higgins, who reported the defeat of the French Army, photographer Robert Capra, who was killed when he stepped on a land mine, and a young French Marine paratrooper who would go on to become one of France's greatest screen idols, Alain Delon.

Born in Sceaux, France, on 8 November 1935, Delon was the only son of Fabien and Edith (Arnold) Delon. His father was a prosperous theater manager and his mother a drug store clerk, but the marriage ended in divorce when Delon was four.

There is confusion regarding the details of his early life, with some accounts stating that he attended a series of private religious academies incurring a consecutive series of expulsions. Others relate that he was cared for by foster parents who lived next to a prison, with the guards' children being his playmates. There is most likely a bit of truth to both stories. The various sources do agree that by the age of fifteen Delon was out of school and living with his mother again, working as an apprentice in her new husband's meat-cutting business.

Despite earning a diploma in cooked meats, Delon was no happier as an apprentice butcher than he had been as a student. When he turned seventeen he persuaded his parents to grant him permission to enlist for three years in the French Marines. Unfortunately, Delon made even less of an accommodation with military discipline than he had with academic discipline. Because of this, and his chronic seasickness, his first year was divided, as he put it, between sickbay and the stockade. However, there was one interruption: he spent three months in the brig for "borrowing" a jeep.

Perhaps as a means to escape the seasickness, Delon volunteered for the paratroopers. The discipline of this elite unit in time corrected his problems with authority. He once stated that while in the Marines, he felt for the first time that he was part of a family: "I had buddies. I had someone to talk to, someone who would listen." Delon was among the French troops sent to combat the Viet Minh insurgents in

Indochina. According to military records, he was involved in fierce fighting, including hand-to-hand combat, before the fall of Dien Bien Phu. Returning to France in 1955, he was honorably discharged from the Marines with the rank of corporal.

Following his discharge, Delon moved to Paris and took an apartment with a friend, supporting himself in a succession of menial jobs. Among the numerous acquaintances he made were several actors and actresses. A trip with his friends to the Cannes Film Festival in 1957 resulted in the offer of a screen test from Henry Wilson, an agent for David O. Selznick. Subsequent meetings with actor Rock Hudson, actress Jennifer Jones, and Selznick himself led to a screen test and the offer of a seven-year contract, the only condition being that Delon learn English. Incredibly, without a bit of experience in the dramatic arts, he was being offered the keys to Hollywood solely on the basis of his dark good looks.

French director Yves Allégret is credited with persuading Delon to remain in France, casting him in his film *Quand la femme s'en mêle* (When the Woman Becomes Confused, 1957). After playing another small part in a comedy directed by Allégret's brother Marc, Delon achieved stardom in his third role, the male lead in Pierre-Gaspard's *Christine* (1958), playing opposite Romy Schneider (to whom he would later be briefly engaged). His next film, *Faibles femmes* (Women Are Weak, 1959), his first film to reach the United States, was met with generally positive reviews.

Delon first attracted international attention in René Clément's *Plein soleil* (1959). The film, which was based on Patricia Highsmith's novel *The Talented Mr. Ripley*, was released in the United States in 1961 as *Purple Noon*. In it Delon played a young bisexual American who murders and then impersonates a wealthy, sadistic friend. (Almost forty years later the film would be remade as *The Talented Mr. Ripley*, with Matt Damon in the Delon role.) His next film, *Rocco and His Brothers* (1960), won special honors at the Cannes Film Festival, as did *L'eclisse* (The Eclipse, 1962) and *Il gattopardo* (The Leopard, 1963).

Delon's Hollywood debut was in *Lost Command* (1966). He performed in three additional films that year, *Once a Thief, Texas across the River,* and *The Yellow Rolls Royce*. He returned to France in 1967, filming Jean-Pierre Melville's cult classic *Le samourai* (The Godson), in which he played the part of an alienated loner, a role he would reprise in several subsequent films.

A career playing gangsters, killers, and sexual deviants caused many to wonder whether life was imitating art or vice versa when Delon and his wife, Nathalie, were investigated by the French police following the discovery of the bullet-riddled corpse of their former bodyguard, Stefan Markovic, in a rubbish dump outside Paris in 1968. The high-profile investigation made tabloid headlines, muddying the reputation of many of France's richest celebrities and most influential politicians, and many predicted the end of Delon's film career. Such was not the case, and he remained one of France's busiest and most popular actors.

Despite, or perhaps because of, performances in films like *Scorpio* (1973), *Zorro* (1975), and *The Concorde—Airport '79* (1979), Delon failed to gain widespread fame or acceptance with American audiences, but he continued to maintain popularity in his native France, earning a César (equivalent to a Hollywood Oscar) for Best Picture in 1976 for *Monsieur Klein*. He was honored with the Best Actor award from the French Academy of Cinema in 1984 for *Notre histoire* (Our Story), named a Commander of Arts and Letters by the Ministry of Culture in 1986, and selected as a member of the Legion of Honor in 1991 by French president François Mitterand.

Denholm Elliott

T hroughout a career that spanned four decades and over 120 films, Denholm Elliott specialized in playing lovable, hapless character parts that often overshadowed the stars of the films in which he was appearing. The consummate Englishman, he could play any role with aplomb, from a bumbling fool to a peer of the realm, and was never above taking minor supporting roles. "When it's a minor or supporting role, you learn to make the most of what you're given. I can make two lines seem like *Hamlet*," he once stated.

Denholm Mitchell Elliott was born in London on 31 May 1922 and was educated at Malvern College, a well-known preparatory school, where he was, by most accounts, a less than stellar student. At the outbreak of World War II, he was a student at the Royal Academy of Dramatic Arts in London. He enlisted in the Royal Air Force Volunteer

(Photofest)

Reserve (RAFVR #1256738) in 1940, just prior to his eighteenth birthday, then returned to London to await being called up. He found the academy empty from the call-up and was getting anxious to go when he received orders to report to Uxbridge for radio operator training. He had a difficult time with the Morse code course and almost washed out, but coaching from a friend pulled him through.

Sent for advanced training at Yatesbury, then Calne, Elliott was promoted to aircraftsman before being assigned to West Malling Airfield, near Kent, where he operated a beacon to light the runway for incoming flights of the Defiant fighters of 141 Squadron.

Elliott earned a promotion to sergeant and assignment as a wireless operator/air gunner posted to Upper Heyford in 1942. He recalled his first bombing mission to targets over Dusseldorf. En route to a target, he picked up a recall order, and the craft turned back, returning home. Other planes that did not pick up the recall continued on to the target, where they found German antiaircraft guns waiting. Many of the flight never returned, and Elliott took pride in the radio skills that had saved his crew.

Transferred to 76 Squadron at RAF Linton-on-Ouse, near York, Elliott flew three missions before his squadron was assigned the target of the submarine base on the German-controlled island of Sylt, off the Danish coast, on 23–24 September 1942. His plane was hit by flak while on a bombing run at three thousand feet. It was the first time Elliott had come under enemy fire, and it was to be his last. Forced to ditch between Sylt and Denmark's Komo Island, two of the crew, Sgt. N. J. Hill, the rear gunner, and Pilot Officer S. E. Groves, the navigator, were killed in action. Squadron leader J. O. Barnard, bombardier Pilot Officer G. T. Lester, flight engineer Sgt. R. Douglass, mid-upper gunner Sgt. R. Gadd, and Elliott were picked up and taken prisoner by the Germans.

Interrogated in Frankfurt for several days, Elliott discovered that his captors knew more about his unit then he did, a not uncommon experience for captured airmen. He ended up in a POW camp, Luft Stalag VIIIB at Lamsdorf, near Breslau, an old POW camp from World War I. With twenty-one thousand prisoners split up into multiple compounds by nationality, it was the largest of the German POW camps. Work parties of prisoners labored on construction sites and farms and in factories, rail

During World War II Elliott flew missions over Germany as a bomber crewman. He was shot down and captured in 1942, then sent to Luft Stalag VIIIB at Lamsdorf, a POW camp near Breslau, Germany. (Denholm Elliott collection)

yards, and mines. The camp also had a dramatics club, and prisoners would put on shows to boost morale and maintain sanity. Eventually Elliott and the other prisoners in the cast went "on tour" to other POW camps. He appeared as Eliza Doolittle in *Pygmalion* and performed in plays like *Journey's End* and *Twelfth Night*.

As the war worsened for Germany and the Russians pressed west into Poland, performances ended for the prisoners, and they were marched west, out of reach of the Russians. Elliott was lucky enough to get a place on a train, but the train was strafed by Allied fighters as it moved west. Interned in a camp near Hanover, he feigned illness and frostbite so as to remain behind in the hospital when the prisoners were moved east following the Allied invasion of Europe. He was liberated by units of British Grenadier Guards and flown home in

March 1945. He was officially discharged from the RAF in 1946, with the rank of warrant officer.

Following the end of the war, Elliott began performing on stage, making his London stage debut in 1946. Three years later he appeared in his first film, *Dear Mr. Prohak*. He made several films in the early 1950s—*The Cruel Sea* in 1952, *The Heart of the Matter* and *The Holly and the Ivy* in 1953, *Lease of Life* and *They Who Dare* in 1954—but continued to perform on stage, debuting on Broadway in 1950.

Elliott first gained international notice in 1964, for his performance with Alan Bates in the film *Nothing but the Best*. Among his more familiar roles are those of Marcus Brody, Harrison Ford's superior in *Raiders of the Lost Ark* (1981)—a role he reprised in *Indiana Jones and the Last Crusade* (1989)—and Elliott Templeton in *The Razor's Edge* (1984), with Bill Murray, a remake of the 1946 film based on the novel by Somerset Maugham.

In 1983, Elliott won his first British Academy of Television Arts and Sciences (BAFTA) Award for his supporting role of Coleman, butler first to Dan Aykroyd, then to Eddie Murphy, in *Trading Places*. Best Supporting Actor BAFTAs followed for *A Private Function* in 1984 and *Defence of the Realm* in 1985. His only Oscar nomination came in 1986 for his role as the freethinking Mr. Emerson in *Room with a View* (1985), a film based on the E. M. Forster novel. The film was also nominated for Best Picture, and Maggie Smith for Best Supporting Actress. Elliott lost out to Michael Caine in *Hannah and Her Sisters*.

Elliott was made a Commander of the Order of the British Empire in 1988. He continued to work in films and on television, including a role as John Le Carre's legendary spy John Smiley in the made-for-TV movie *A Murder of Quality* (1991). He succumbed to AIDS-related tuberculosis at his home in Ibiza, Spain, on 6 October 1992. In 1995, Susan Elliott, his wife of thirty years, published *Quest for Love,* in which she wrote of his career, his bisexuality, and their open marriage.

★

Peter Finch

P eter Finch was the only actor to be awarded a Best Actor Academy Award posthumously. He won the prestigious award for his rousing portrayal in *Network* of Howard Beale, a frenzied television anchorman turned "mad prophet of the airwaves." During the film Beale would often open the studio window and shout out into the darkness, "I'm mad as hell, and I'm not going to take it anymore." He became a national rallying symbol for viewers who had become fed up with the inanity of television programming. The film was made in 1976, and one cannot help but wonder why we have not heard similar cries in the night since then, considering the state of American television programming today.

Peter Finch was born in London on 28 September 1916. He was registered as Frederick George Peter Ingle-Finch on 5 February 1917.

(Photofest)

He was born while his mother's husband, George Ingle-Finch, was serving overseas with the Royal Artillery during World War I. Upon Captain Ingle-Finch's return from the war, a question arose between him and his wife regarding the boy's paternity. The result was that Ingle-Finch began legal proceedings and divorced his wife, Alicia Gladys Fisher, on the grounds of adultery on 15 March 1920. He named Maj. Wentworth Edward Dallas as a correspondent and gained custody of the boy. Many years later Finch stated that his mother had told him that his real father was a Scottish major named Campbell.

Finch was taken to France at an early age and stayed with an aunt in Paris, where he learned about eastern philosophies while attending primary school. At the age of ten, after a brief visit with other relatives in India, he was sent to live with his grandparents, Laura and George, Sr., in Sydney, Australia. He attended North Sydney Inter High School during the depression, leaving school in 1934. He initially worked as a reporter-trainee on the Sydney newspaper the *Sun*. There followed a host of other odd jobs—waiting tables, working as a ranch hand, washing dishes, and driving a taxi—before he got his first break in "show business" upon answering an ad for a vaudeville comedian's straight man. Finch enjoyed the company of actors, whom he described as "cheerful idiots."

By 1935, Finch was acting on tour and had begun working in radio. Indeed, his excellent voice would make him the country's leading radio actor in years to come. When Australia declared war on Germany on 3 September 1939 in support of the British empire, Finch was granted an exemption from military service since he was needed to act in propaganda films and make war bond tours, activities deemed essential to the war effort. Uncomfortable with not being in uniform ("I didn't see why I should stay out when everyone else had to go"), Finch enlisted in the Australian Army on 2 June 1941, was assigned to the artillery as Gunner Finch #NX26035, and was sent to an antiaircraft regiment.

After a brief period of basic training, Finch's unit was en route to the Middle East aboard the *Queen Mary* as a part of Specialist Group No. 2. The Australian Army sent three divisions to the Middle East (the 6th, 7th, and 9th) and one to Malaya (the 8th). Finch was sent to Palestine, then to Syria, where he joined the Allied occupation

Finch in *The Red Tent* (1971). He enlisted in the Australian army in 1941 and was sent to the Middle East as an antiaircraft gunner. Eventually he returned to Australia to help defend the country against Japanese aerial attacks. (Photofest)

forces. The Vichy French elements and German agents that held Syria had been defeated by Allied ground forces in early June 1941, and Finch's 7th Division was sent in to stabilize the area. The unit was next sent to reinforce British forces in Singapore and was en route to Sumatra when the city fell on 15 February 1942. Later in the year the unit was ordered to return to Australia on board the ammunition ship *Niger Storm* to help defend the country against Japanese aerial attacks. Finch manned an antiaircraft gun in Darwin, enduring numerous Japanese air raids. To relieve the stress, he organized shows, informally called "Finch Follies," using talent drafted from local units.

In December 1942, Finch, now a sergeant, was granted leave for a bond tour during which he met his future wife, Tamara Tchinarova. The two married on 21 April 1943. His leave was extended so that he could appear in the film *Red Sky at Morning* (1945). Upon completion of the film and his leave, Finch was given the choice of returning to his old unit or accepting a transfer to an entertainment unit. He elected to return to his antiaircraft outfit, but after a period of boredom and inactivity he requested a transfer to an entertainment unit.

Finch was transferred to the Army Amenities Unit No. 12 at Pagewood in Sydney. His old commanding officer for the antiaircraft unit said, "I'm deeply sorry you're going. You were a bloody awful soldier, but you did make me laugh." Finch made propaganda films such as *The Rats of Tobruk* (1944) and formed an entertainment troupe. In August 1945 he was admitted into a hospital with a severe case of urethritis and fatigue. He was discharged as a sergeant on 31 October.

After the war, Finch formed a repertory company, the Mercury Players, who performed on stage across Australia. Sir Laurence Olivier saw a performance while on tour in Australia and invited Finch to London, where he became a protégé of the famed actor. With Olivier's help, Finch found work on the London stage and was also cast in several films. His first starring role, opposite Elizabeth Taylor in the Paramount movie *Elephant Walk* (1954), gained him notice in Hollywood.

He earned five British Academy of Film and Television Arts (BAFTA) Best Actor Awards: for *A Town Like Alice* (1956), *The Trials of Oscar Wilde* (1960), *No Love for Johnnie* (1961), *Sunday, Bloody Sunday* (1971), and *Network* (1976). His other notable films include *Kidnapped* (1960), *The Flight of the Phoenix* (1965), *Far from the Madding Crowd* (1967), and *Lost Horizon* (1973).

Peter Finch died quite suddenly at age sixty-one from a massive heart attack while sitting in the lobby of a Beverly Hills hotel waiting to continue his tour promoting *Network*.

★

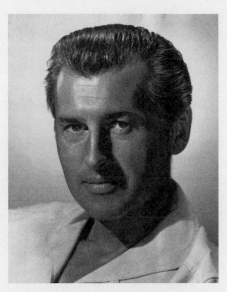

Stewart Granger

Romantic, swashbuckling Stewart Granger was, with James Mason, the top British box office draw of the 1930s and 1940s, his acting career well established at the outbreak of World War II. When England went to war, Granger enlisted in the Gordon Highlanders and underwent training at Aberdeen as a private. He had had officer training while in college and was familiar with drilling. Being an actor, he exuded confidence and a gung-ho attitude that was somewhat at odds with his true feelings. His sergeant major soon became frustrated with his recruits and barked, "Ye've joined the Brigade of Heelanders, and Heelanders ye'll be if it kills me, but I've the feeling it might kill ye furst."

Granger remembered nothing very interesting about his Army life, with the exception of a few incidents that remained with him long after the war ended. He recalled meeting his first Nazi when a captured bomber crew was brought to Aberdeen and placed under guard there to await transfer to an interrogation center. The crew had been captured by the Royal Navy. However, the Navy had not done the job entirely alone. In those days, whenever a German plane was shot down over the English Channel, there would be a race between fishing boats and Navy ships to get to the downed crewmen first. The Luftwaffe (German Air Force) habitually strafed defenseless fishing boats, and the fishermen were eager to exact their revenge. Whereas the Royal Navy would hold the Germans for interrogation, the fishermen would hold their heads under water.

Granger, now a lance corporal, was ordered to bring food to the holding quarters of the Luftwaffe pilot, who angrily swept the food from the table. Granger's sergeant took one look and ordered that another tray of food be brought to the prisoner. When the food was brought in, the sergeant ordered Granger and the others in the room to do an about-face. "Behind us," Granger relates in his autobiography, "we heard a sort of stifled gurgle, the sound of a plate smashing, and odds and ends hitting the floor. On the order to turn about again, to our joy we saw this arrogant bastard with sausages sticking out of his collar and fried egg all over his face. 'He tripped,' our sergeant told us. 'He's not hungry now, are you ducks?'" Granger's sergeant was not one to fool with; his father had been killed in the Battle of the Somme during World War I, and he himself had been wounded at Dunkirk.

Granger also recalled an incident in which he thought he had performed a heroic deed against the enemy. German aircraft had attacked a British freighter near the coast, and the craft was able to beach itself. A salvage team went to work repairing the ship, since at the time all such vessels were vital to the war effort. Granger was sent with his unit to mount a beach patrol and protect the ship, and every morning and evening the Luftwaffe would send over a Stuka dive bomber to try to destroy the ship. His unit had one Bren gun with one magazine of ammunition, which was in short supply at the time. The weather was bitterly cold, owing to the winds blowing off the North Sea; all of the soldiers were heavily dressed. One morning after tea Granger suddenly had to relieve himself, and he disappeared behind one of the blocks of cement that studded the beach to defend against a possible invasion.

Granger with American actress Ava Gardner during filming of *Bhowani Junction* (1956). He enlisted in the Gordon Highlanders and was eventually commissioned and posted to the Black Watch before being shipped overseas to the North Africa campaign. Granger eventually developed health problems that invalided him out of the army. (Photofest)

Just as he got his trousers down, he heard the distinct diving scream of a Stuka. With that he grabbed the gun and started blasting away at the plane, all the while tripping over layers of trousers, pajama bottoms, and long johns. As it dropped its bomb and slowly passed him, he fired the entire magazine at the aircraft. To his amazement, the plane caught fire and crashed into the sea. He jumped up and down in elation as his buddies ran to congratulate him. While they were celebrating, a Spitfire flew over them doing a victory roll. Deflated, Granger hoped that maybe one of his bullets had found its mark.

Granger was next ordered to Cruden Bay to fend off a possible attack by the Germans from Norway. The members of his unit underwent training and were assigned defensive positions, although the weaponry they were given would hardly have warded off a German landing force. They were provided with old World War I–era Enfield rifles with about ten rounds of ammunition each, Bren guns with one magazine each, and 3-inch mortars with six shells per mortar.

In early 1941, Granger went through officer's training at Morecambe Bay and upon commissioning was posted to the Black Watch. He was posted to the 6th Battalion, a famous unit whose officers and men wore the French croix de guerre as shoulder flashes. The award had been bestowed on the 6th for its courageous combat action against German forces during World War I.

As the men of the 6th awaited orders to be sent overseas, they were visited by their colonel-in-chief, who turned out to be the queen herself (now the queen mother). After they had paraded past her, she addressed them with the words, "My Highlanders," which drew a roar from the assembled troops. Granger remembered the moment, with the men waving wildly at her. They all would have died for her then and there.

When the 6th Battalion was ordered to join the North African campaign, the hard training, forced routed marches, sleeping in ditches, and Army cooking proved too much for Granger's nervous stomach. He developed an ulcer and was hospitalized. Despite a diet of citrate of milk, his condition was deemed chronic, and he was invalided out of the Army. He found out later that his battalion had suffered horrific casualties in North Africa.

Following his discharge, Granger returned to movie acting and went on to appear in numerous films in Britain, and in 1950 he caught the attention of Hollywood movie makers. Over the next twenty-five years he performed in some fifty motion pictures, including *King Solomon's Mines* (1950), *Scaramouche* (1952), *Bhowani Junction* (1956), *Harry Black and the Tiger* (1958), and *The Wild Geese* (1978). He became a U.S. citizen in 1956. The last of his three wives was actress Jean Simmons. Stewart Granger died in 1993.

★

Alec Guinness

<hr />

Alone British landing ship (HMS LCI 124) hit the beach at Cape Passero lighthouse on 9 July 1943. It was the beginning of Operation Husky, the invasion of Sicily. Tumultuous seas pushed the stern of the craft at such an angle that the two hundred soldiers it carried could not use the ramps alongside the ship's bow to go ashore. Using ropes, they lowered themselves into the surf and scrambled across the beach to take up their positions. No enemy opposition was encountered, much to the surprise of the commander of the landing craft.

Suddenly, from out at sea, a thunderous barrage began, and explosions erupted half a mile inland. The commander, Sub-Lt. Alec Guinness, had expected this shelling an hour earlier. Puzzled, he watched as several of the soldiers he had landed returned to the beach, along with a few terrified Italian prisoners. An hour later the sub-lieutenant stood before an angry Royal Navy commander, who demanded to know why he had been so late in landing. Guinness, Royal Navy Volunteer Reserve (RNVR) and commander of No. 124, replied that he had not been late. In fact, he had been the first to land his men. The officer did not believe him. He asked just what Guinness did as a civilian. Acting, replied the latter, adding that although it had not been part of his orders, he had in fact landed first, leading all others. He had landed on time, he insisted, at the exact spot specified in his orders. "And you will allow me to point out, sir, as an actor, that in the West End of London, if the curtain is advertised as going up at 8:00 p.m., it goes up at 8:00 p.m. and not an hour later, something that the Royal Navy might learn from."

World War II records confirm that Alec Guinness brought ashore the first invasion force at Sicily. However, things had not gone according to plan. Hours before the invasion, Guinness had maneuvered his landing craft alongside a troopship to pick up two hundred soldiers from the 5th Battalion of the Black Watch (Royal Highland Regiment). Boarding the soldiers became extremely hazardous, owing to heavy seas that damaged the ship's bow ramps. They became useless for transporting the troops to the landing craft. The soldiers had to jump into the LCI as waves lifted the craft alongside the troopship. In the confusion of getting the men safely on board, Guinness missed the signal to all ships that the invasion had been postponed by one hour. Once free of the troopship, he headed straight for land just left of the Cape Passero lighthouse. He was eight miles away from his landing beach point in his assigned quadrant passing other landing craft that were circling off the beach. He beckoned them to follow, but none did.

The legendary stage and screen actor was born Alec Guinness de Cuffee in London on 2 April 1914. During his teen years he attended Pembroke Lodge boarding school, Southbourne. His early desires to participate in school plays were dashed when the headmaster informed him that he was not the acting type. He was not given his first chance to act until 1932, when he attended Roxborough, Eastbourne, where he completed his formal education. Guinness was given the role of the breathless messenger in *Macbeth,* an appearance for which he prepared himself by running around the school's playing field six times before making his entrance.

Upon graduating at age eighteen, he joined a London advertising agency as an apprentice copywriter and layout artist. But the work bored him; he felt completely unsuited for it. Instead he decided to pursue his true interest, acting. He arranged to work with actress Martita Hunt, who after their first session declared that Guinness had no talent at all. But the fledgling actor persevered and persuaded her to coach him. Within a few years, her work had paid off. Guinness was awarded a two-year scholarship to the Fay Compton Studio of Dramatic Art and soon made his stage debut in a walk-on part. Lacking the means to continue at the studio after his scholarship ran out, he left the school. During the next year he landed small parts in less than notable stage plays. Still he persevered.

Alec Guinness's big break came in 1934, when famed actor John Gielgud cast him as both Osric and the third player in *Hamlet*. By 1936 he had found regular work with the Old Vic Company, playing roles in plays by Shakespeare, Shaw, and Chekhov. In 1938 he married actress Merula Salaman, with whom he continued to share his life until his death in 2000. They had one son.

When Britain and Germany went to war on 3 September 1939, the recently married Guinness enlisted in the Royal Navy. An actor friend had originally offered to get him into an Army antiaircraft unit, but he quickly learned that it was already overstaffed with actors and thus his presence would not be welcome. He was processed in a disused school in North London, passed the necessary tests, and within ten weeks was ordered to HMS *Raleigh* for training as an ordinary seaman. A commission lay in the offing if he could satisfactorily complete several training courses at various stations. Following his *Raleigh* tour, Guinness received further training at Lancing College and HMS *King Alfred* at Brighton.

In 1942 he went before a commissioning board to determine his suitability as an officer. Standing at rigid attention before ten seated admirals, he overheard their initial comments about his training, which were not too encouraging: "Navigation not too good" . . . "Mathematics very poor" . . . "Gunnery marks are appalling." There were a few good marks: "Drill, good" . . . "Smartness, yes." After a few questions, he was curtly dismissed. The admirals' notes were collected. The senior officer had written on the back of his notepad,

"Probably more to him than meets the eye." Shortly thereafter, Alec Guinness received his commission, designated sub-lieutenant in the Royal Navy Volunteer Reserve. He would not see his new wife and son for the next two and a half years, time that he served mostly in the Mediterranean theater.

Guinness may not have seen enough of his family, but he did have pals he could talk to, including actor Peter Bull, whom he had befriended during training. Both became Royal Navy officers and LCI captains, and they ran into each other regularly. Bull became a character actor after the war, best known in America as the German gunboat captain in *The African Queen* (1951) and the Russian ambassador in *Dr. Strangelove* (1964).

In the summer of 1942, Guinness was appointed first lieutenant of a tank landing craft, HMS TLC 24, on Loch Fyne, Scotland. The greasy, rusty ship underwent naval exercises up and down the loch all through the cold fall, with a first lieutenant who never did learn exactly what his duties were, though he found the commanding officer friendly enough. Nor, during his three months on board ship, did he get to know the crew. Eventually Guinness and other Royal Navy officers were ordered to the United States to take command of new large infantry landing craft, or LCI(L)s, that were being built in a shipyard on Quincy Bay, near Boston. Traveling on the *Queen Mary,* they crossed from the gray, cold, blacked-out British Isles to the dazzling lights of New York City.

Four days later, Guinness was posted to Asbury Park, New Jersey, there to await the completion of his new command. Within a few weeks he was contacted by a fellow British thespian, Terence Rattigan, who was in New York on leave from Royal Air Force bomber duties. His play, *Flare Path,* was to be produced for Gilbert Miller's theatrical company. There was no one available to play the juvenile in the production. Rattigan insisted that Guinness play the role. He had cleared the way through the British ambassador, who had been given permission to use Guinness by the British Admiralty, since the play offered an excellent propaganda opportunity. Guinness appeared in the production for eight weeks before returning to Asbury Park and his ship.

Finally commissioned, the ship, No. 124, was prepared for its Atlantic voyage. Both officers and men were green at this point, and

British infantry landing ships (LCIs) and troops going ashore during Operation Husky, the invasion of Sicily. Guinness, a sub-lieutenant in the Royal Navy Volunteer Reserve, commanded an infantry landing ship, HMS LCI 124, and was first to land troops at Sicily. (U.S. Naval Historical Center)

Guinness feared they might sink the ship before arriving at their eastern Atlantic destination. He was pleasantly surprised when they managed to complete the first task, taking on fresh water and diesel oil. Each fluid went into its proper tank successfully. Next they attempted to take the craft out for a trial run, in the process of which several starboard stanchions were snapped off and a wooden jetty severely cracked. No. 124 gained such a reputation for mishaps, in fact, that other LCIs upon sighting it often put out their fenders and fled in mock terror.

Problems dogged them from their first trip, Boston to New York. Arriving as darkness descended, No. 124 turned into the East River and a dense fog, meaning they would have little chance of mooring in the ship's assigned slip. Ships were forbidden to anchor in the river, so Guinness, in order to avoid a possible collision, decided to sidle up to an embankment and make fast to whatever solid structures they could find along the shore. They finally located and tied up to a lamp post and a park bench. After warning his quartermaster to observe the tide during the night and let out slack as necessary, Guinness retired to his cabin.

The next morning when he went on deck, a nightmarish scene awaited him. The park bench was in the water, the lamp post was bent over at a 90-degree angle, and the ship had moved away from the shore. The quartermaster had fallen asleep. Guinness started his main engines, severed the lines, and slipped away from the area to scurry to the ship's proper berth.

With a slightly more seasoned crew, No. 124 crossed the Atlantic in sixteen days with a small armada of British ships, docking at the town of Djidjelli, Algeria, in the spring of 1943. Djidjelli was located 120 miles west of Algiers, and it offered a peaceful respite for the officers and their crews. The enemy lay to the north across the Mediterranean in Italy, Greece, and France, and no one knew of the operations that lay ahead. All they knew was that an Allied invasion of one of these countries would take place sometime soon.

A week after their arrival, all LCI commanders were summoned to a top-secret meeting to study photographs taken by a submarine. Beaches were clearly marked by lettered quadrants, but there was no identification of where the photos had been taken. Guinness noticed on one of the prints a small white lighthouse with a barely visible number 58 underneath. Thinking that perhaps they could identify the lighthouse's location, after the briefing Guinness and another skipper went back to No. 124 and began studying the two volumes of *The Mediterranean Pilot,* a mariner's mapping of Mediterranean sea lanes that included navigational aids and lighthouse locations. Only one lighthouse was listed as being fifty-eight feet high. It was located at Cape Passero, on the southeastern tip of Sicily.

On 9 July 1943, when Guinness opened his secret orders an hour after leaving Malta, he was not surprised to read that the beaches at Cape Passero were in fact among the shore areas where the invasion of Italy would take place. The invasion force of troopships, destroyers, cruisers, and an aircraft carrier rendezvoused a few miles west of the southern tip of Sicily. Guinness took aboard his landing force and landed them at Cape Passero.

He had to wait ten days following the invasion before a destroyer could tow his beach-entrenched No. 124 seaward. The crew relaxed on the beach, swam, and played games. One man developed an acute toothache, and Guinness decided to walk with him to the nearest Army camp. During their short journey, the two plodded through a large bean field, taking care not to damage it. They found the camp, and the ailing crew member was attended to. The dentist asked how they had got to the camp. Guinness told him, and the shocked doctor gave them the news that they had just walked through a minefield. Practically every bean plant had been booby-trapped. They stuck to the shoreline on their return trip.

At sea once again, the LCI was used to ferry men and supplies to the Sicilian ports of Syracuse, Augusta, and Catania. By September 1943 the Italians had signed an armistice, and Guinness was assigned to the Adriatic. There he supplied arms and munitions to the Yugoslav partisans.

Guinness lost his ship on one of these missions, during a terrifying storm en route from Barletta, Italy, to the Yugoslav island of Vis. As they neared the island, they were caught in a hurricane that had blown in from the southeast, across the Mediterranean from Egypt and Libya. Fighting thrashing seas that engulfed the ship in thirty-foot waves and gales that made control almost impossible, Guinness took the LCI into the harbor at Termoli, on the Adriatic coast of Italy. No. 124 was already severely damaged, and a huge wave lifted it onto rocks forward of an abandoned tank landing craft. Amazingly unhurt, the crew scrambled ashore and awaited the end of the storm, which raged for three days. Damaged beyond repair, LCI 124 was eventually turned into a concrete jetty at Termoli.

With his ship gone, Guinness was ordered to Malta. Here he took command of LCI(L) 272, and he settled into a daily routine of ferrying supplies to Yugoslav partisans, then returning to Italy with their wounded. But they were not always welcome in Yugoslav ports. Often when they dropped off supplies marked as gifts from the United Kingdom or United States, young partisans appeared with pots of red paint with which they painted over the UK/USA markings, "From the

USSR." Soon thereafter Rome fell, and two days later, on 6 June 1944, Allied forces stormed ashore at Normandy.

The rest of the year proved uneventful for Guinness and his crew, who continued their runs in the Adriatic. Only once did they bring supplies to partisans on the Greek mainland. One gray morning while docked in Barletta, Italy, Guinness received a signal that his relief was on the way. After his replacement arrived and the turnover procedures had been completed, Guinness traveled to Naples for shipment back to England.

Arriving on board a troopship at Liverpool, the actor was reunited with his family in London. He was shocked at the devastation of the grand city he remembered. The sound of air-raid sirens, which he had not heard in a long time, alarmed him more than anything he had experienced in the Mediterranean. After four weeks of desk duty in Southampton, he made a few forays across the channel in a tank landing craft. The war with Germany was soon over.

While he awaited demobilization, Guinness was asked to play the role of Herbert Pocket in a film to be made of Charles Dickens's 1860 novel *Great Expectations,* which was released in 1946. Guinness's commanding officer gave him permission to accept the offer, and so the actor returned to his profession. It was the beginning of a new, and soon to be illustrious, movie career.

Previously a theater actor, Guinness continued to appear on the London stage through the 1970s, building a reputation as one of England's finest dramatic actors. Over the years he has received numerous awards for his brilliant, often mesmerizing performances. Before *Great Expectations,* he had appeared on screen only once, as a walk-on in the movie *Evensong* (1934). But the Dickens story would be followed by many film roles showcasing his versatility and comedic talent. Between 1946 and 1992 he appeared in more than fifty movies. In 1957 he won an Oscar for his brilliant performance in *The Bridge on the River Kwai.* Queen Elizabeth knighted him in 1959 for his achievements on stage and screen. And in 1980, Hollywood awarded him an honorary Oscar "for advancing the art of screen acting through a host of memorable and distinguished performances." Recent generations of moviegoers remember him best as the wise old spiritual warrior Obiwan Kenobi in *Star Wars* (1977), *The Empire Strikes Back* (1980), and *Return of the Jedi* (1983).

For his military service Guinness received five campaign stars and war service medals: the 1939–45 Star, the Atlantic Star, the Italy Star, the Defence Medal, and the War Medal. He was appointed a Commander of the Order of the British Empire in 1955. In 1994 he was appointed a Companion of Honour, a very prestigious honor usually limited to top scientists and artists, though others have received it also (e.g., Winston Churchill). There are only about fifty current holders of the order. He also had the rare distinction of being awarded honorary Doctor of Letters degrees from both Oxford and Cambridge, as well as a Doctor of Fine Arts degree from Boston University.

Cedric Hardwicke

Cedric Hardwicke was born in Lye, Stourbridge, Worcester, England, on 19 February 1893, the son of a physician. Although his father had a strong dislike for the theater, Hardwicke was allowed to enroll in the Royal Academy of Dramatic Arts. After graduating and working in a series of small productions, he made his London stage debut in 1912. World War I interrupted a promising career, and it was not until he returned from France following the end of the war that he began to distinguish himself on the stage and screen—so much so that he was knighted by King George V in 1934. In 1938 he moved to Hollywood, where he established himself as a leading character actor. In the years that followed he alternated between Hollywood and England performing in plays and film

(Photofest)

Hardwicke as Archdeacon Dom Claude Frollo in *The Hunchback of Notre Dame* (1939). Hardwicke saw combat in World War I and survived the Battle of the Somme, a five-month struggle resulting in more than a million British and German casualties. At the end of the war, he was the last officer to leave the war zone in France. He performed in more than eighty pictures during his career, and he was knighted in 1934 by King George V. (Photofest)

productions. In the course of his lengthy theatrical career he appeared in over eighty movies.

During World War I he was commissioned as a second lieutenant in the infantry, then was transferred to the cavalry and assigned to the 34th Division. Horse power dominated military life during that war. Horses transported men, food, ammunition, and fuel. When rail lines stopped, the horses took over. Hardwicke's unit arrived in France in January 1915. He was tasked with transporting food and other commodities from railheads to front-line troops.

Hardwicke participated in the disastrous Battle of the Somme, which lasted five months. Two million men engaged in fierce combat on a thirty-mile front between Amiens and Péronne. No strategic gain was made by either side, and the cost was almost unimaginable. On the first day of fighting alone, the British Army suffered sixty thousand casualties, twenty thousand killed; Germans losses were six thousand killed and wounded, two thousand taken prisoner. After surviving the Somme, Hardwicke was transferred to the Northumberland Fusiliers in early 1918. From then until the end of the war he was one of the many British soldiers who fought in the trenches along the Western Front.

Upon his return to England in November 1918, Hardwicke served an additional three years in the Army. He was subsequently ordered to put together theatrical productions to bolster troop morale. His troupe, "Concert Parties," traveled to various bases in England and France. His last duty station was at the British General Headquarters at Saint-Pol, France, where he assumed the position of camp commandant. It was at Saint-Pol that the body of the Unknown Warrior was selected. Hardwicke recalled, "I never walk past the Cenotaph without recollecting the night when I mounted guard with other officers over the body of the Unknown Warrior until dawn in the makeshift chapel at Saint-Pol. It was an unforgettable experience."

Hardwicke was the last British officer to leave the war zone. His final duty was to haul down the Union Jack, which he kept in his possession for the rest of his days.

After seven years of service Hardwicke was discharged from the Army as a captain and returned to the theater to begin a long, illustrious theatrical career. His first movie after the war was *Nelson* (1926), and his last appearance was in the British film *The Pumpkin Eater* (1964), with James Mason, Peter Finch, Anne Bancroft, and Maggie Smith; many film critics said that he had saved his best performance for last. His other notable films include *The Moon Is Blue* (1943), *The Keys of the Kingdom* (1945), *The Desert Fox* (1951), and *Around the World in Eighty Days* (1956).

Hardwicke was married twice to actresses, Helena Pickard in 1928 and Mary Scott in 1950. Both marriages ended in divorce. He had one son from the union with Mary Scott. Sir Cedric Hardwicke died of emphysema in New York in August 1964. He is said to have once stated, "I can't act. I have never acted. And I shall never act. What I can do is suspend my audience's power of judgment till I'm finished."

★

Rex Harrison

Rex Harrison will perhaps always be remembered for his portrayal of Professor Henry Higgins in the stage play and movie *My Fair Lady*. The charming, elegant, and rather blasé actor won a Tony Award for his stage performance and an Oscar and New York Film Critics Best Actor award for the follow-on film released in 1964 in which he co-starred with Audrey Hepburn. However, by 1964 Harrison had appeared in numerous plays and films on both sides of the Atlantic that had established him as a first-rate performer. His more notable films include *Anna and the King of Siam* (1946), in which he played opposite Irene Dunne; *Cleopatra* (1963); *The Yellow Rolls Royce* (1964), with Shirley MacLaine; *The Agony and the Ecstasy* (1965); and *Doctor Dolittle* (1967).

Reginald Carey Harrison was born in Lancashire, England, on 5

(Photofest)

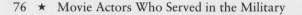

Harrison with Audrey Hepburn in *My Fair Lady* (1964). Trained as a radar operator, he was commissioned and assigned to the 10th RAF Group in Benson. (Photofest)

March 1908. He attended Birkdale Preparatory School and made his stage debut at Liverpool College in 1924 in *Thirty Minutes in a Street*. He made his film debut in 1929, but his first love was the stage. By 1936 he was acting before the camera during the day and before stage audiences at night.

After England entered World War II in 1939, Harrison immediately tried to enlist with director Carol Reed in the Inns of Court Cavalry Regiment. The colonel of the regiment told them that they should return home to await call-up orders. They tried to enlist in other units and almost took positions with a Royal Air Police unit, but decided they did not want to spend the war guarding airfields. After Dunkirk, and the end of the "phony" war in June 1940, Harrison and Reed were accepted into the Chelsea Home Guard.

Accepted into the Royal Air Force in February 1942, at the RAF station at Uxbridge, Harrison underwent a six-week officer training course. He received no special treatment and was remembered as a "regular bloke." He had hoped to train as a pilot, but his eyesight did not meet minimum standards (in fact, it was rumored that he had a glass eye). He was subsequently trained as a radar operator and was commissioned as a flight officer in the RAF Volunteer Reserve. Following his commissioning, he was assigned as a flight control liaison officer with the 10th RAF Group at Benson in January 1943. He was tasked with the safe return of damaged bombers flying back from night raids over Germany. He would coordinate between Flight Command (who were in radio contact with the aircraft) and ground or air/sea rescue units. Harrison provided Flight Command with the bombers' positions as they staggered home.

In late 1943 and early 1944, Harrison was transferred to the 11th Group Headquarters at Uxbridge and was seconded to an RAF film unit. He performed in Noel Coward's film *Journey Together* (with Edward G. Robinson and Richard Attenborough), but his work ended up on the cutting-room floor. He continued to serve with the 11th Group Headquarters, returning to his duties as a flight control liaison officer. In 1943, Harrison and his wife, actress Lilli Palmer, were at home when a bomb fell fifteen feet from their house, partially destroying it. Both were unharmed. A second house to which they had moved barely missed being destroyed by a German V-2 bomb in 1945. That bomb landed in the front yard of their new home, causing only minor damage.

High command, having decided that Harrison was most valuable for raising morale in film, honorably discharged him as a flight lieutenant in the spring of 1944. He entertained British and American troops in Germany and across Europe until the war ended in May 1945.

Following the end of the war Harrison continued to perform mostly on the stage but managed to work in over fifty films. Only a month before his death at eighty-two he starred on Broadway opposite Glynis Johns and Stewart Granger in Somerset Maugham's *The Circle*.

Harrison was married six times. His first wife, Collette, was the mother of his son Noel Harrison. He was wed to actress Lilli Palmer, mother of his son Carey, from 1943 to 1957. He married actress Kay Kendall, several years his junior, in 1957. Unbeknownst to her, she was terminally ill at the time of their wedding, and Harrison continued to shield her from this fact until her death in 1959. His fourth wife was actress Rachel Roberts; his fifth wife was Elizabeth Harris; and in 1979 he was married for the last time, to Mercia Tinker.

Rex Harrison was knighted by Queen Elizabeth in 1989. He died in New York City on 2 June 1990.

Laurence Harvey

He played such legendary figures as Romeo in *Romeo and Juliet* (1954) and Col. William Travis in *The Alamo* (1960). He starred with some of the greatest screen legends of the century (John Wayne, Elizabeth Taylor, Paul Newman, Frank Sinatra) and worked under some of the industry's greatest directors (Alfred Hitchcock, Orson Wells). He won a Best Actor Oscar nomination for his role as the amoral social climber Joe Lampton in *Room at the Top* (1959). But it was as Sgt. Raymond Shaw, in the John Frankenheimer adaption of the 1959 Richard Condon novel *The Manchurian Candidate* (1962), that Laurence Harvey will forever be remembered.

Larusschka Mischa Skikne was born in Joniskis, Lithuania, on 1 October 1928. His parents, Ber and Ella Skikne, moved the family to

(Photofest)

Johannesburg, Union of South Africa, in 1934, when Harvey was five, to escape persecution for their Jewish faith.

Harvey grew up in Johannesburg and was educated at the Earl of Athlone High School and Meyerton College. At best an apathetic student, he much preferred perfecting his English by attending American films in the afternoon at the local cinema. These films exposed Harvey to a greater view of the world, a world he was eager to explore.

With the war raging in Europe, Harvey attempted to enlist in the Royal South African Navy in 1942, at the age of fourteen. A letter from his mother to the naval authorities advising them of his true age resulted in his expeditious discharge. Undeterred, Harvey again enlisted in 1943, this time in the South African Army. His deception regarding his age went undiscovered, and he is credited with service in the North African and Italian campaigns. He finished his military service in 1946 while assigned to an entertainment unit.

Following his discharge, Harvey went to England and enrolled in the Royal Academy of Dramatic Arts. He left after three months to join a classical repertory theater in Manchester, despite an offer from Warner Brothers Pictures to attend a studio school at $100 a week, a generous salary at the time.

Harvey later said that it was by "playing the classics" on stage that he learned his craft and perfected his command of language. In 1947 he accepted his first film role, in *House of Darkness* (1948), produced by International Pictures, a small British production company. That same year, using the proceeds from the film, he returned to South Africa where he and his parents were naturalized as South African citizens and British subjects.

A series of British films followed, including *The Man from Yesterday* and *Man on the Run* in 1949, *Cairo Road* in 1950, *The Scarlet Thread* and *There Is Another Sun* in 1951, *I Believe in You* and *Women of Twilight* in 1952, and *Innocents in Paris* in 1953. Although hoping for a career in comedy, a supporting role in a 20th Century Fox film, *The Black Rose* (1950), with Tyrone Power, elevated his status as an actor with leading-role potential.

This image was confirmed in 1954, when he was cast as the male lead in *Romeo and Juliet,* his first starring role. The film won an award at the Venice International Film Festival that same year.

Harvey in his most memorable film, *The Manchurian Candidate* (1962). Born in Lithuania and raised in South Africa, Harvey enlisted in the South African army in 1943. He served in North Africa and Italy before his discharge in 1946, while he was assigned to an entertainment unit. (Photofest)

Following two more American films, *King Richard and the Crusaders* and *The Good Die Young* (both 1954), Harvey returned to England to make *I Am a Camera* (1955); *Storm over the Nile* (1956), a remake of Alexander Korda's *Four Feathers* (1939); and *The Silent Enemy* (1958).

Harvey's breakout role was as Joe Lampton in the internationally acclaimed *Room at the Top* (1958), released the following year in the United States. The film won Oscars for Best Screenplay and Best Actress (Simone Signoret) as well as nominations for Best Picture, Best Actor (Harvey, who lost to Charlton Heston in *Ben Hur*), and Director (Jack Clayton). It also won the British Academy of Film and Television Arts (BAFTA) Award for Best British Film, Best Film from any Source, and Best Foreign Actress (Signoret), as well as nominations for Best British Actor (Harvey and Donald Wolfit) and Best British Actress (Hermione Baddeley).

Harvey's success opened up opportunities for roles in *The Alamo* (1960), with John Wayne and Richard Widmark, which was also nominated for the Best Picture Oscar in 1961; *Butterfield Eight* (1960), with Elizabeth Taylor, who won the Academy's Best Actress award for her performance; and *Walk on the Wild Side* (1962), with Barbara Stanwyck, Ann Miller, and Jane Fonda.

Also in 1962, Harvey was cast in a role that would earn him screen immortality, as Sgt. Raymond Shaw in *The Manchurian Candidate*. The story concerns a returning Korean War hero scheduled to receive the Medal of Honor for his actions in saving his platoon. In reality, his platoon was captured and brainwashed, and Shaw was programmed to assassinate a presidential candidate. With its themes of brainwashing, McCarthyism, assassination, and political intrigue, the movie has been called everything from a "political paranoia thriller" to "sophisticated political satire." It offended both the far-left and far-right elements of the American political landscape, and it was pulled from the theaters after former Marine Lee Harvey Oswald assassinated President John F. Kennedy in Dallas in November 1963. Critics wrote that Harvey's performance stole the picture from co-stars Frank Sinatra, Janet Leigh, and Angela Lansbury. The film, unavailable for twenty-five years, was re-released in 1997 to critical praise and has become a cult classic.

Harvey continued to make films as well as perform on television and with the Old Vic Company in London, but by 1967 his health was failing and his work had become sporadic. He was married three times, to Margaret Leighton in 1957, Joan Cohn in 1968, and Pauline Stone in 1972. Laurence Harvey died of colon cancer at his home in Hampstead, England, on 25 November 1973, at the age of forty-five.

Jack Hawkins

Noted for playing figures of authority, such as Major Warden in *The Bridge on the River Kwai* (1957) and General Allenby in *Lawrence of Arabia* (1962), John Edward "Jack" Hawkins was born in London on 14 September 1910. From his earliest days, Hawkins seemed destined for the stage. He attended his first school at age five, where he joined the choir. He made his London theatrical debut at age twelve, playing the Elf King in a production of *Where the Rainbow Ends*.

When he was fifteen, an influential family friend assisted Hawkins in getting admitted to the prestigious Julia Conti School of Drama, and three years later he made his American stage debut in the Broadway production of *Journey's End*. He returned to London and married his leading lady, Jessica Tandy, in 1932. They would divorce ten years later.

(Photofest)

Hawkins with Alec Guinness and William Holden in *The Bridge on the River Kwai* (1957). At the outbreak of World War II, Hawkins volunteered for the Royal Welsh Fusiliers. He went on to officer training, was commissioned a second lieutenant, and posted to the 1st Battalion of the Royal Welsh, an amalgamation of Welsh regiments sent overseas to India. He was later assigned to ENSA and at the war's end was in charge of entertainment for the entire Southeast Asia Command. (Photofest)

Although Hawkins did some work in silent films, his first "real" film role is considered to be his appearance in Alfred Hitchcock's sound version of *The Lodger* (1932). He made more than a dozen films in the next eight years, including *A Shot in the Dark* (1933), *Autumn Crocus* (1934), *Peg of Old Drury* (1935), and *Murder Will Out* (1939).

After the outbreak of World War II in September 1939, and following the evacuation of Dunkirk, Hawkins volunteered as a private in the Royal Welsh Fusiliers. Following basic training at Whexham, Cheshire, he was selected for training as an officer and was shipped off to Officer Training Corps at Pwllheli, North Wales.

Shortly after being commissioned a second lieutenant, Hawkins was given leave to appear in the propaganda film *Next of Kin* (1942). Upon his return to duty he was posted to the 1st Battalion of the Royal Welsh, an amalgamation of the Welsh regiments, headquartered at the Cheltenham race course. The unit was sent overseas to India, and Lieutenant Hawkins was assigned as executive officer of a Bren gun platoon, as part of the 2nd Division.

After producing a show, *Cross Keys* (named for the division's insignia), Hawkins's unit followed the Fourteenth Army on its drive into Burma, and Hawkins received a promotion to captain. With his ability at production recognized, he was released from his unit for duty supervising the Indian and Far East branch of the Entertainments National Service Association (ENSA), with a promotion to major.

Hawkins eventually gained responsibility for coordinating entertainment for all British forces in India. As the Fourteenth Army drove the Japanese back, the entertainers were close behind the advancing British forces. While with ENSA in India, Hawkins met an actress, Doreen Lawrence, whom he married in 1946. Before leaving the Army when the war ended, Hawkins was in charge of entertainment for the entire Southeast Asia Command. He spent his final months of duty traveling throughout India, Burma, Malaya, and Ceylon.

Advised by his friend Alexander Korda to return to film acting, Hawkins accepted a three-year contract, beginning a film career that would include performances in seventy movies. His first starring role to win acclaim was his portrayal of a World War II British convoy captain in the film adaptation of Nicholas Monsarrat's bestselling novel *The Cruel Sea* (1953). He starred with Alec Guinness in *The Prisoner* (1955) and again in *The Bridge on the River Kwai* (1957). He finished the 1950s in style, with roles in *Ben Hur* and *The League of Gentlemen* (both 1959).

Hawkins traveled the world in the 1960s, going to the Middle East to star with Alec Guinness and Peter O'Toole in *Lawrence of Arabia* and to Africa for *Zulu* (1964) with Michael Caine, and worked with Richard Attenborough in *Guns at Batasi* (1964). He then went to the Far East for *Lord Jim* (1965), again with Peter O'Toole.

Throat cancer led to a laryngectomy (removal of the larynx) in 1966, which resulted in the loss of his voice. He continued to appear in minor roles, however, and learned to mouth his lines, which were dubbed in later. He appeared in *Oh! What a Lovely War* (1969), *Kidnapped* and *Nicholas and Alexandra* (both 1971), and *Young Winston* (1972).

Despite four nominations for Best Actor by the British Academy of Film and Television Arts (BAFTA), Hawkins never won the award. His last performance was as Justice Gilroy in the television mini-series *QB VII*. He died at his home in London in 1973.

★

Sessue Hayakawa

A man of many talents, Sessue Hayakawa was an accomplished director, actor, writer, and watercolor artist, as well as a college football star and a Zen Buddhist priest. But he is remembered by most American moviegoers for his role as a Japanese Army officer Colonel Saito in the 1957 film *The Bridge on the River Kwai*, which starred Alec Guinness and William Holden.

He was born Kintaro Hayakawa at his father's estate near the town of Nanaura on the island of Honshu, Japan, on 10 June 1889, the youngest of five children. From an early age Hayakawa's ambition was to be an admiral, and his father, governor of Chiba prefecture, raised him under the strict warrior code of Bushido and encouraged him in his desire to pursue a naval career.

Hayakawa entered the Naval Preparatory School in Tokyo and was

(Photofest)

a student at the start of the 1904 Russo-Japanese war. An average student, he excelled in athletics and martial arts. Upon completing his course of instruction in June 1908, he was scheduled to enter the Naval Academy, but an injury sustained while diving to win a bet resulted in his hospitalization for severely damaged ear drums. This mishap caused his subsequent disqualification and dismissal from the academy in December 1908.

Despondent over his loss of face and his uncertain future, he attempted seppuku, or hari-kari, but survived despite multiple self-inflicted stab wounds. After a period of recovery, during which he meditated and worked to master the principles of Zen Buddhism, and a chance meeting with Americans in May 1909, he decided to visit the United States.

Overcoming his father's objections, Hayakawa went to America and enrolled in a political science course of study at the University of Chicago. He played football on the university's team until he was disqualified for excessive fouls. (He was known to use judo on his gridiron opponents.) In 1913, after graduating from the university, he returned to Japan to commence a political career. However, before sailing for home he was distracted by a stage production he saw in the Little Tokyo section of Los Angeles. He decided to stay in America and joined a Japanese theater group. He was discovered by Thomas H. Ince while performing with a troupe in San Francisco and hired at $500 a week to star in the 1914 movie *Typhoon*.

The following year Hayakawa was cast in Cecil B. de Mille's film *The Cheat* and received glowing reviews from movie critics. His star began to rise rapidly. By 1918 he had his own production company, and within a few years he became a millionaire. His popularity in the United States soared. He worked with such American stars as Douglas Fairbanks and Mary Pickford, was invited to the White House by President Warren G. Harding, and gave a command performance for Britain's King George V and Queen Mary in the 1930s.

Although he made films in his native country, his pro-Western lecture tour of the Far East in 1932 won him no friends in Japanese military circles. In 1937 he went to Paris to film *Yoshiwara*, and he remained in France to work with Erich von Stroheim in *Macao, l'enfer du jeu* (Gambling Hell, 1942). He was in Paris at the start of World

War II and learned that he was unwelcome in Japan because of his opposition to the warlord faction in power. When Germany occupied France in 1940, Hayakawa found himself in the uncomfortable position of being a pro-Western Japanese national in an occupied country. After the Japanese attack on Pearl Harbor and the U.S. declaration of war on Japan, he could not return to the United States, because he was an enemy national. Fleeing to England was not possible for the same reason. He subsequently rejected the opportunity to collaborate with the Germans in France. Suspected by both sides, Hayakawa remained in France throughout the war, supporting himself by selling watercolors he painted.

Although he kept a low profile, he cooperated with the local French underground when possible and was present for the liberation. He welcomed Allied troops and entertained them in his home. He was relieved to be accepted as "a famous American movie star." He remained in France making films until he was permitted by American authorities to return to the United States in January 1949 for a role in *Tokyo Joe,* which starred Humphrey Bogart and Florence Marly, and later *Three Came Home* (1950), with Claudette Colbert.

In the early 1950s Hayakawa returned for a time to Japan, where he was chosen as a candidate for the Zen Buddhist priesthood in recognition of his work in producing the play *The Life of the Buddha* (1949). He was ordained as a Zen Buddhist priest in the early 1950s. He returned to Hollywood in 1956 to work in the film *The Bridge on the River Kwai.* The movie, released in December 1957, won seven Academy Awards, including Best Picture, Best Director (David Lean), and Best Actor (Alec Guinness), and Hayakawa was nominated for an Oscar for Best Supporting Actor.

Sessue Hayakawa died in Tokyo on 23 November 1974, at the age of eighty-four.

★

Anthony Hopkins

P erhaps always to be known in the years to come for his performances as Dr. Hannibal "the Cannibal" Lecter in *The Silence of
the Lambs* (1991) and *Hannibal* (2001), this brilliant actor has
become a top box office draw because of these captivating films. Hopkins has always been a superb actor, but playing Hannibal has brought
him fame and fortune perhaps beyond what he ever envisioned. There
will probably be a third Hannibal movie, since the character seems to
have enthralled audiences as few have done over the last decade.

Phillip Anthony Hopkins was born on 31 December 1937 in Margam,
South Wales. He was the only child of baker parents who sacrificed to
send him to a private boarding school. He was sent to Cowbridge in
Glamorgan, and Hopkins recalls "loathing" the place and its rigid class
system. After leaving school he worked as a laborer in a steel foundry.

(Photofest)

Hopkins as Hannibal Lecter in *Silence of the Lambs* (1991). Inducted into the British army in 1958, he was assigned to the Royal Artillery at Oswestry-Shropshire, England. (Photofest)

In 1956, in the midst of the cold war, Hopkins became eligible to be called up for the draft. He tried to avoid National Service by feigning deafness, but no one was deceived, and he was inducted into the British Army in February 1958. Hopkins became Gunner Hopkins #23449720, Royal Artillery, at Oswestry-Shropshire. In April he was posted to the clerk's school at Woolwich, London, hoping to be sent to Cyprus upon completion of training, which would earn him some embarkation leave. However, in May he was assigned as a typist at Regimental Headquarters, 16th Light Antiaircraft Regiment, RA, at Bulford Camp, earning 28 shillings a month. Hopkins found his work difficult because the colonel he worked for had a habit of using no consonants when he spoke. Hopkins couldn't understand a word the man said and could barely decipher the handwriting in the letters he gave him to type.

One day he was given the task of typing out a regimental report, a

Board of Enquiry. The sixteen-page report had to be typed perfectly, and Hopkins labored throughout the night to ensure that it would be absolutely flawless. Upon its completion he read and reread it and was satisfied that no one could quibble with his work. After it was checked over by Staff Sergeant Little early the next morning, he was told to take the report over to the Stores and run off two dozen copies. Completing his task, he tore up the original and returned to his office, where he was told to take the copies into the adjutant for signature. The adjutant asked if Staff Sergeant Little had checked the report. Hopkins replied that he had. The adjutant signed the first copy and stopped, then asked when Hopkins was to go on leave. Hopkins replied, "Next week." The adjutant replied, "Thank God for that. Could you send the chief clerk in? You've rolled all these on blotting paper!" The papers had to be signed in ink, so the whole lot had to be done over again.

Hopkins made friends with several of the senior Welsh soldiers and had a relatively easy time of it in the service. In February 1960, at the end of two years' service, he was discharged as a corporal. Upon his release he auditioned for the Liberty Theatre in Manchester and was hired as stage manager. After a stint with the Nottingham Playhouse, he attended the Cardiff College of Drama, and in 1961 he joined the Royal Academy of Dramatic Arts, where he trained until 1963.

After witnessing Hopkins's second audition, Laurence Olivier asked him to join the National Theatre Company (NTC), which specialized in Shakespeare and the classics. Hopkins remained with the NTC from 1966 until 1972. In 1974 he journeyed to America, where he appeared on Broadway in *Equus* and remained to direct the Los Angeles production. Hopkins stayed in America appearing in films such as *Victory at Entebbe* (1976), made for television; *The Lindbergh Kidnapping* (1976), also made for television, with Hopkins as Bruno Hauptmann; *A Bridge Too Far* (1977); *The Elephant Man* (1980), as Frederick Treves; *The Hunchback of Notre Dame* (1983), as Quasimodo; *The Bounty* (1984), as Captain Bligh; *Howards End* (1992), with Vanessa Redgrave; *The Remains of the Day* (1993), with Emma Thompson; *Nixon* (1995); *Titus* (1999); and *Hearts in Atlantis* (2001).

Hopkins's awards include an appointment as a Commander of the Order of the British Empire and a Best Actor Oscar for *The Silence of the Lambs*. Although knighted in 1993, he had to relinquish his knighthood when he became a U.S. citizen in 1994. He now lives in California.

★

Leslie Howard

A ctor, director, and producer Leslie Howard is best remembered
for his portrayal of the character Ashley Wilkes in the 1939
blockbuster *Gone with the Wind*, considered by many today
to be the greatest film ever made. The epic garnered eight Oscars:
Best Picture, Best Director, Best Actress, Best Supporting Actress, Best
Screenplay, Best Color Cinematography, Best Art Direction, and
Best Editing.

Leslie Howard always played Leslie Howard—an idealistic, dreamy,
and upright gentleman. At a time in the 1930s when American actors
such as James Cagney and John Garfield were being cast in rugged, vio-
lent parts in films depicting the dark side of society, Howard led a group
of sixty-six "aristocratic" British actors onto the American screen in
films that favored brains over brawn. His cohorts—Herbert Marshall,

Howard as Capt. Ashley Wilkes in *Gone with the Wind* (1939). At the start of World War I Howard enlisted in the British army and was commissioned as a second lieutenant in the cavalry. He was sent to France, where he saw combat for three months in Passchendaele. In June 1943, he was lost while flying as a civilian passenger in a commercial airliner en route from Algiers to London. German fighters shot the plane down over the Bay of Biscay. (Photofest)

Charles Laughton, Sir Cedric Hardwicke, and others—displayed a level of quiet sophistication that greatly appealed to American audiences. Howard was perceived as the perfect English gentleman, something of a romantic poet and a keen intellectual. He was rarely cast as a villain and usually played characters who were courageous and noble.

Leslie Howard Stainer was born in the Forrest Hill section of Lon-

don on 3 April 1893. Of Hungarian descent, he grew up in Vienna.
After attending Dulwich College in London, he enlisted in the British
Army at the start of World War I. He was assigned to the cavalry
despite having little experience with horses. After several months of
training as a cavalry officer, he was commissioned a second lieutenant.

Howard was assigned to a battalion of the Northamptonshire Yeomanry Regiment stationed near Colchester. He found life in the regiment easy and enjoyed long rides in the English countryside. During
that period he met and married Ruth Martin, a female employee in the
local recruiting office. They eventually had two children, a son,
Ronald, and a daughter, Leslie Ruth.

By 1916 there had already been over sixty thousand British war-
inflicted casualties, and Howard's unit was ordered to prepare for shipment to France. Upon arrival they were sent to the Western Front,
where cavalry units were of little use in the mud-soaked battlefields
and trenches. By the time the United States entered the war in April
1917, Howard had already sustained almost three straight months of
constant combat in Passchendaele, and he was returned to England
with a severe case of shell shock for which he was invalided out of
the Army and medically discharged that year.

Before joining the Army, Howard had worked at a bank and then
became an actor. He made his film debut in 1914 in *The Heroine of
Mons*. Following his release from the Army he returned to acting and
made his stage debut in 1917 in *Peg o' My Heart*.

For the next two decades he made numerous stage and film appearances. His more notable films include *Of Human Bondage* (1934); *The
Scarlet Pimpernel* (1935); *Pygmalion* (1938), for which he won a Best
Actor award at the Venice Film Festival; and *Intermezzo* (1939), which
co-starred Ingrid Bergman in her first English-speaking role.

Howard returned to England when war was declared in September 1939. He had been spending a considerable amount of time in
Hollywood acting, producing, and directing films. He continued with
his work once back in England and in 1940 began a series of broadcast talks, "Britain Speaks."

In 1943, while en route from Lisbon to London aboard BOAC 777,
a British Oversea Airways flight, Howard was killed when Nazi fighters shot the aircraft down over the Bay of Biscay. Controversy con-

tinues to surround the incident, as some believe that British intelligence officials knew from their Ultra communications intercepts that the Germans planned to shoot the plane down, but failed to warn the crew for fear of compromising the knowledge that they had broken the German codes. The German interceptors suspected that Winston Churchill was among the passengers. In fact, Churchill's double, Alfred Chenfalls, was aboard the plane.

Howard's last movie was *The First of the Few* (1942), which he directed and in which he played the role of Reginald Mitchell, the designer of the Spitfire.

Trevor Howard

Born Trevor Wallace Howard-Smith on 29 September 1916 in Cliftonville, Kent, a suburb of the seaside resort of Margate, the son of Arthur Howard-Smith and Canadian-born Mabel Wallace, Trevor Howard spent his early childhood in Ceylon, where his father worked as an insurance underwriter with Lloyd's of London. Little is known about his father except that he came from a large family and was a dedicated stamp collector. During his tour in Ceylon he returned to England on leave every three years, and his absence made him seem more like a distant relative than a father to Howard and his younger sister, Merla Lagiere. Mabel Wallace, on the other hand, was a remarkable person. When just a young woman she left Canada to study nursing in the United States. Upon graduation she became a private nurse and was employed as such by wealthy fami-

(Photofest)

lies. When her patients went abroad, Mabel and her two children traveled with them, and she quickly acquired a thirst for travel.

When Howard was five years old, Mabel scheduled a trip back to England with stops along the way. At the end of their extended journey, Howard was to be enrolled in a proper school in England to begin his education. Mabel and the children boarded an ocean liner at Colombo and waved farewell to Arthur standing on the dock. It would be two years before they saw their father again. The ship made port calls at Singapore, Japan, the Philippines, Hawaii, and San Francisco before docking at Los Angeles, where they enjoyed a long stay with family friends. The great San Francisco earthquake of 1906 occurred while they were in Los Angeles, and Mabel left the city for San Francisco to offer her nursing services. Years later, when she told of her experiences in the devastated city, Howard would listen politely but not really believe the tales she told. It was only after her death that he found out that her remembrances were well documented.

Howard attended school briefly in Los Angeles before Mabel took the children by train to Canada to visit her relatives. After a year of staying with Wallace-clan members in Ottawa, Toronto, and Brandtford, Ontario, Mabel's wanderlust took them to New York City to see the new wonder of the world, the Empire State Building. The family finally ended their long journey by crossing the Atlantic to England. Howard was just eight years of age when his mother enrolled him in the junior school at Clifton College in Bristol. His mother and sister then headed back to Ceylon.

When Howard was fifteen, an aunt living in America invited him to New York City for a visit. Prohibition was the law of the land in America, but Howard, in the company of older cousins, was soon visiting speakeasies and listening to jazz, which became a lifelong passion. The holiday finally came to an end, leaving its indelible mark: he wanted to be a jazz musician. He tried the drums, but with little success. He liked to perform but was not sure where this desire would lead.

While at Clifton, Howard was a mediocre student but excelled in sports. As graduation neared, his mother returned to England to join in the festivities of her son's last days at Clifton. While watching Howard play in a soccer game prior to his graduation, Mabel found herself sitting next to Howard's English teacher, a Mr. Garrett. They

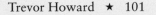

Howard with Michael Caine in *The Battle of Britain* (1969). He was inducted into the Royal Corps of Signals in 1940 and posted to the 2nd South Staffordshire Regiment in Bulford, Wiltshire, England. (Photofest)

struck up a conversation and agreed that Howard had not given either of them a hint of what he intended to pursue after he left Clifton. However, Garrett had seen something in Howard that others had missed during his many classroom Shakespearean readings. Garrett sensed that Howard had a natural talent for the theater, and he suggested that the young man attend the Royal Academy of Dramatic Arts. Somewhat taken by surprise, his mother readily agreed, since the only other recourse for her son was perhaps a stint in the Army. Howard enrolled in the academy in 1932, and thus began his illustrious theatrical journey.

Howard performed so well at the academy that he was selected best actor in his class and was granted a rare academy scholarship for his second year of study. While still a student, he made his professional debut in *Revolt at the Reformatory* at the Gate Theatre. A number of roles in the theaters of London's West End followed his graduation, and he was working as an actor with the Harrogate White Rose Players at the Stafford Memorial Theatre in London when Great Britain went to war in September 1939.

Howard immediately attempted to enlist in the Royal Air Force but was rejected. He was also rejected by the Army for the same reason given by the RAF: the number of volunteers exceeded the ministry's ability to process men, and priority had to be given to those in the reserves. Howard was told to return home and await his call-up papers.

Howard resumed acting but was unaware of the fact that when his call-up papers arrived, the two ladies who ran the Harrogate White Rose Players destroyed them, not wanting him to leave the company. He was made aware of this fact only upon being arrested by the police for evasion. He was inducted into the Royal Corps of Signals as a private on 2 October 1940.

After basic training, Howard was sent to a railway signals unit but was returned by the unit when he failed to show any aptitude during follow-on training. A posting to coastal artillery yielded the same results. Howard finally volunteered for the infantry ("I knew I could walk") and was sent to an officer cadet training unit in Dunbar, Scotland. Between maneuvers, he organized cadet productions and plays. He graduated on 3 October 1942 and was commissioned a second lieutenant in the infantry.

Posted to the 2nd South Staffordshire Regiment in Bulford, Wiltshire, Howard soon grew bored with the routine: "I was at least an officer, but I don't think I behaved like one at all." Anxious for action, he volunteered for the Red Berets, the embryonic airborne regiment. What followed was a year of almost constant training in airborne operations, assault courses, and physical conditioning. Howard recalled, "They couldn't afford to have new officers in charge of platoons unless they were absolutely first class. If there was any risk . . . you failed the physical."

Howard failed a physical and was invalided out of the Army on 2 October 1943, three years to the day after his induction. Later accounts of his war service, including his 1988 obituary in the *New York Times,* have him parachuting into Norway and Sicily and earning the Military Cross in the process. Per Howard, "It was a load of crap for the sake of building up my image as some kind of hero." The truth is, Howard felt cheated for not getting the opportunity to "do his bit" after wasting three years.

Upon his discharge, Howard returned to acting and a role in his first film, *The Way Ahead* (1943), in which he played a naval officer. He achieved stardom in his third film, Noel Coward's *Brief Encounter* (1946). A long and distinguished film career followed, with roles in films like *The Third Man* (1950), *Around the World in Eighty Days* (1956), *Mutiny on the Bounty* (1962), *Von Ryan's Express* (1965), *The Battle of Britain* (1969), *Superman* (1978), and *Gandhi* (1982).

During his thirty-year career, Howard appeared in seventy-two movies, twenty-eight stage plays, and twenty-four made-for-TV productions. He received a Best Actor award from the British Academy of Film and Television Arts (BAFTA) for *The Key* (1958) and a Best Actor Emmy for *The Invincible Mr. Disraeli* (1963), and he was nominated for a Best Actor Oscar for *Sons and Lovers* (1960).

Howard married British actress Helen Cherry in 1944. After enjoying a long, illustrious theatrical career and forty-four years of marriage living in quiet domesticity, one of the greatest British film actors of his generation died in his sleep in a London hospital on 7 January 1988.

Klaus Kinski

Legendary for his abuse of interviewers and for the excesses of his private life, Klaus Kinski chose roles in his life that rivaled the often bizarre roles he played on the screen. A stage actor by preference, he claimed for years to have chosen his film roles solely for the fees they offered.

Klaus Kinski was born Nicolaus Gunther Nakszynski on 18 October 1926 (some accounts say 8 October, most only 1926) in the Sopot section of Danzig (now Gdansk, Poland), a free port city under the auspices of the League of Nations. His father was a pharmacist and failed opera singer, and his mother was the daughter of a local pastor. His family was very poor, and with the depression, his father was unable to make a living and so moved the family to Berlin in 1931. The family took German citizenship, and Kinski's early years must

(Photofest)

have been filled with images of National Socialism as he grew up in the heart and capital of Nazi Germany.

Drafted into the Wehrmacht (German Army) sometime in 1943, Kinski saw no action until the winter of 1944, when his unit was sent into Holland on a "training exercise." His obituary in *Variety Magazine* states that "he was wounded his second day of combat in Holland . . . and was taken prisoner by the British."

Kinski's own recollections of that time as presented in his autobiography *Kinski Uncut* bring a different perspective. It *was* his second day in combat, but Private Kinski had made the decision to desert on his first day, and had done so while out on patrol. Slipping away from the others, he went into the woods. He was caught by the Germans, court-martialed as a deserter, and sentenced to death. He subsequently escaped and went into hiding in the woods, only to stumble upon a British patrol, which fired on him, wounding him in the arm. Treated by British surgeons, Kinski was interrogated, then transported west for shipment to a POW camp in England.

The ship he was aboard was torpedoed by a German sub while crossing the English Channel, but Kinski was safely offloaded and transferred to a POW camp at Colchester, Essex. It was here that he first performed on stage, taking parts in the camp shows the prisoners put on to maintain morale. He recalled being cautious, as even in the camp, fervent Nazi prisoners were still to be feared.

Following Germany's surrender and the end of the war there in May 1945, German POWs anticipated their release and return home. When Kinski heard that sick prisoners would be returned first, he did everything he could to try to qualify. He stood outside naked during icy nights. He ate cigarettes. He drank urine. It was all to no avail. He remained healthy, and in captivity, for one year and four months. Finally, in 1946, he was released.

Kinski returned to a Berlin far different from the one he had left. The once modern city was now a collection of bombed-out ruins. His father had died during the war, his mother had been killed in the street during an Allied fighter attack, and the city was now occupied by victorious Allied troops. Kinski spent his first year in Berlin living in an unheated theater. He took minor roles on stage and delivered poetry recitals in cabarets across the city, which proved enormously popular, and he began taking small roles in films.

Compiling a complete filmography for Kinski would be an impossible task, since he made between 170 and 200 films. Nevertheless, it seems certain that his first appearance was in a German film, *Morituri* (1948), followed by *Das Kalte Herz* (The Cold Heart, 1950) and *Decision before Dawn* (1951), his first American film. His films bear titles as diverse as *The Counterfeit Traitor* (1962), *Kali Yug, Goddess of Vengeance* (1963), *Naughty Cheerleaders* (1970), and *The Beast Kills in Cold Blood* (1971). Many of them were made in Europe and are unfamiliar to American audiences. Kinski's better-known films include *A Time to Love and a Time to Die* (1958), in which he played a Gestapo officer; *Doctor Zhivago* (1965); the Sergio Leone spaghetti western *For a Few Dollars More* (1966); and *The Wild Geese* (1984). Others include Billy Wilder's comedy *Buddy-Buddy* (1981) and *The Little Drummer Girl* (1984), with Diane Keaton.

Most critics agree that Kinski did his most memorable work during his fifteen-year collaboration with German director Werner Herzog. His first film with Herzog, *Aguirre: The Wrath of God* (1972), was followed by *Woyzeck* (1978); *Nosferatu the Vampyre* (1979), a remake of F. W. Murnau's 1921 horror classic; and *Fitzcarraldo* (1982), in which he replaced Jason Robards in the role of the Irish-born dreamer.

Kinski continued working into the late 1980s in films that included *Kinski Paganini* (1989), which he also wrote and directed. His 1989 autobiography *Ich Brauche Liebe* (Everything I Need Is Love) infuriated many, including his daughter, actress Nastassia Kinski, who filed a libel suit against him. It was soon withdrawn.

Kinski died of natural causes at his home in Lagunitas, California, on 24 November 1991. He was once quoted as saying, "I am my own God, my own jury, my own executioner. . . . Heil Gunther."

Hardy Krüger

T all, blond, and blue-eyed, Hardy Krüger built a film career on portraying German soldiers in countless war movies, including Field Marshal Erwin Rommel in the television mini-series *War and Remembrance* (1989).

Born Franz Eberhard August Krüger on 12 April 1928 in Berlin, he grew up during the turmoil accompanying the rise of National Socialism during the late 1920s and early 1930s. Like most German youth of his era, he was probably a member of the Hitler Youth. Some believe that Krüger enjoyed favored status with Josef Goebbels, the Nazi minister of propaganda. Not surprisingly, his Aryan good looks helped him secure his first screen role in the propaganda film *Junge Adler* (Young Eagles), at the age of sixteen. The plot of the movie concerned a member of the Hitler Youth working with other young men

(Photofest)

Krüger as a German officer in *A Bridge Too Far* (1977). Krüger was born in Berlin in 1928. At the age of sixteen, he was drafted into the Wehrmacht's Brandenburg Division, a group of old men and young boys Hitler sent against the Allies in a last desperate attempt to win the war. Krüger saw action on the Rhine and the Austrian Tyrol. When the war ended, he tried to hitchhike back to Berlin, but he was captured and then escaped—three times. He finished the war as an American POW. (Photofest)

in a Heinkel aircraft plant, learning the virtues of discipline and sacrifice as they toiled for the Fatherland. By 1944, when the film was made, celluloid was the only place where Germany was still winning the war.

By 1945, Krüger was a soldier in the Brandenburg Division, a group comprised of young boys and old men sent by Hitler as a last desperate attempt to stem the Allied advance. Krüger finished the war as an American POW. Upon his release, he worked as a carpenter and held bit jobs in small theaters, working into a spot as an extra at the Hamburg Playhouse, where he was "discovered" by Wolfgang Liebeneiner. Eventually he moved up to bigger stages, first in Hanover, then in Hamburg, Berlin, Munich, and Stuttgart.

In 1949, Krüger returned to film work in a series of romantic movies like *Kätchen für Alles* (Katrina for All, 1949) and *Das Mädchen aus der Südsee* (The Girl from the South Sea, 1950). His popularity reached national levels with the release of *Illusion in Moll* (Illusion in a Minor Key) in 1952, and he made a number of films in his native Germany before earning international acclaim for his role portraying Oberleutnant Franz von Werra in the 1957 British film *The One That Got Away*. Von Werra was the only German prisoner of war taken to Britain during World War II who escaped from British POW camps and got back to Germany.

Other notable film appearances include *Hatari* (1962); *The Flight of the Phoenix* (1965), which earned him a Best Supporting Actor Golden Globe nomination in 1966; and *Barry Lyndon* (1975). He also appeared in numerous action films like *The Secret of Santa Vittoria* and *The Battle of Neretva* (both 1969), *A Bridge Too Far* (1977), and *The Wild Geese* (1978).

During the 1970s and 1980s, Krüger began directing television documentaries in Europe while continuing to appear in films, including *The Inside Man* (1984) and *The Spy Who Never Was* (1986). From 1961 to 1973 he was proprietor of the Momella Game Lodge in Tanzania. At present Krüger continues to direct television documentaries. His daughter, Christiane Krüger, is a stage and film actress.

Charles Laughton

Famed British actor Charles Laughton went to war at the age of eighteen. He enlisted in the British Army as a private during World War I and despite his class and education turned down the opportunity to be commissioned, stating, "I did not want to command . . . to take responsibility for other people's lives."

Laughton was sent to France early in 1918, assigned as part of the Royal Huntingdonshire Rifles, and was posted to Vimy Ridge. He never talked publicly about what happened there, but official records indicate that the Royal Huntingdonshires were involved in a fierce bayonet engagement. His wife, Elsa Lanchester, whom he married in 1929, recalled that Laughton told her about the battle one night and said that he had had to stab men to death. Laughton had been a very sensitive nineteen-year-old at the time, and that horrifying experience

A British army private during World War I, Laughton was assigned to the Royal Huntingdonshire Rifles in 1918 and posted to Vimy Ridge in France, where he saw combat and was gassed. During World War II he was too old for service, but he made numerous contributions to Britain's war effort. Laughton is shown here conducting a radio broadcast during a war bond drive that raised $298,000 in bonds. (From *Movie Lot to Beachhead* [1945], by the editors of *Look* magazine)

haunted him for many years. A few days before the end of the war he was gassed, and for the rest of his life he periodically suffered from severe rashes on his back. The gas also affected his larynx and trachea, and he feared that he might lose his voice. However, his throat healed within a few days of the incident, and he was demobilized early in 1919.

Charles Laughton was born in Scarborough, Yorkshire, England, on 1 July 1899. He was the oldest of three boys born to an Irish mother and innkeeper father. All three boys were born in their parents' inn, the Victoria Hotel. He attended Stoneyhurst but left the school without taking the London certificate that would have facilitated his acceptance at a university. He then enlisted in the British Army.

Following his discharge in 1919, Laughton returned to Scarborough and his family's newly acquired inn, the Pavilion Hotel. His father sent him to London to work at the Claridge to learn the hotel business. He worked as a bill clerk, control clerk, and cashier's clerk. During his off hours he spent all his money on tickets to theatrical productions at various city theaters. He saw one show, *Chu Chin Chou*, thirteen times.

After a year he returned to the Pavilion and refurbished the hotel to make it more appealing to the traveling public. As a result of his efforts, the hotel flourished. While working at the Pavilion he directed and performed in amateur productions for the Scarborough Players. Laughton next enrolled at the Royal Academy of Dramatic Arts in London at the age of twenty-four. The following year he was awarded the Bancroft Gold Medal, the academy's highest award, for his performance in *The Merry Wives of Windsor*.

In 1929 Laughton made his feature film debut, in *Piccadilly*. He moved to Hollywood in 1933 and signed a contract with Paramount. A year later he won a Best Actor Oscar for *The Private Life of Henry VIII*. That film and *Rembrandt* (1936) were produced in England, but the remainder of his films were made in the United States.

Laughton was too old for military service during World War II, but his contributions to the American war effort were unstinting. In 1942 he met two GIs who were recuperating at Birmingham General Hospital in the San Fernando Valley. He was subsequently invited to the hospital to do readings from Shakespeare and the Bible for the patients. At the end of his performance before a packed auditorium he recited the Gettysburg Address. The reception he received was overwhelming, and he returned to the hospital almost weekly until the war ended. He was also a regular on war bond tours. In Cincinnati he told a reporter, "This tour is the least I can do. I was in the last war and I know that the soldier and the sailor need encouragement and the feeling that those at home are behind him." He conducted war bond drives on radio and on one occasion raised $298,000 in bonds during a seventeen-hour broadcast.

In the late 1940s Laughton toured in programs of great readings from literature as a member of the First Drama Quartet (with Agnes Moorehead, Charles Boyer, and Cedric Hardwicke). In 1952 he produced and directed the Broadway production of *The Caine Mutiny Court Martial* and a few years later directed the film *The Night of the Hunter* (1955).

Laughton is probably best remembered for his performances as Captain Bligh in the 1935 film *Mutiny on the Bounty,* which starred Clark Gable and Franchot Tone, and as Quasimodo in *The Hunchback of Notre Dame* (1939), with Maureen O'Hara. Other films of note include *Witness for the Prosecution* (1957) and *Advise and Consent* (1962). Charles Laughton died in December 1962.

Christopher Lee

Perhaps the only man in the history of cinema to portray the Frankenstein monster, Count Dracula, the Mummy, Fu Manchu, and both Sherlock Holmes and Sherlock's brother Mycroft, Christopher Lee has enjoyed a long and successful film career spanning fifty-five years, specializing in pictures with titles like *Dr. Terror's House of Horror* (1965), *The House That Dripped Blood* (1970), and *The Creeping Flesh* (1972). Together with fellow British actor Peter Cushing, with whom he made twenty-two films, Lee can be credited with restoring the popularity of horror films.

Born Christopher Frank Carandini Lee in Belgravia, London, on 27 May 1922, he was the son of a professional soldier and an Italian contessa. His father, Lt. Col. Geoffrey Lee, served in the 60th King's Royal Rifle Corps and was decorated for gallantry in the Boer War and

(Photofest)

World War I. The elder Lee commanded Australian troops (46th Battalion, 12th Brigade of the 4th Australian Division) at the Battle of the Somme, where his actions earned him a Croix de Guerre, presented personally by Marshal Ferdinand Foch.

Lee's mother, Contessa Estelle Marie Carandini di Sarzano, was from one of the oldest and most distinguished families in Europe, tracing her lineage as far back as Charlemagne. She was a noted beauty and the subject of numerous paintings.

Educated at Summer Fields Preparatory School, Lee took a scholarship to Eton and Wellington colleges, where he studied classical Greek and Latin and gained his first exposure to theatrics. In college he excelled in squash, rugby, football, hockey, fencing, cricket, and especially golf, a passion that continues to this day. He is the only actor made a member of the Honorable Company of Edinburgh Golfers, the oldest golf club in the world, founded in 1744.

Early in 1941 two events occurred that changed the direction of Lee's life: the death of his father and his enlistment in the Royal Air Force Volunteer Reserve (RAFVR). He enlisted as an aircraftsman second class and pilot candidate on 5 May 1941, just weeks before his nineteenth birthday. He passed on the opportunity to join his father's regiment in favor of the chance to learn to fly.

Lee was ordered to report to the RAF barracks at Uxbridge, where, as he recalled in his autobiography, *Tall, Dark, and Gruesome,* he excelled in marksmanship and drill but had difficulties with other aspects of military life. "I couldn't swear, although I was willing to learn, and I was opposed to drinking much, because drink tended to make people drunk. These distinguishing features, as well as my accent which was unlike theirs, made the fellows look at me askance."

Assigned to No. 4 Elementary Training Wing at Paignton, Lee was posted to West Kirby near Liverpool, where he took classes in navigation, Morse code, and weaponry. This was followed by a six-week voyage aboard the *Reina del Pacifico,* en route under convoy to Capetown, South Africa, for flight training. (During the war, British pilots took flight training in Canada, Africa, and the United States, far from the dangers of German pilots.) The troops were well received in South Africa and neighboring Southern Rhodesia, and Lee recalls numerous invitations to parties and hunts.

Lee in Alexandria, Egypt, in 1942. He enlisted in the Royal Air Force Volunteer Service in 1941 and underwent flight training in South Africa but was eventually grounded because an optic nerve problem affected his sight. He was later trained as an intelligence officer and assigned to 260 Squadron, serving subsequently with Special Air Service and Special Operations Executive. (Christopher Lee collection)

The pilots trained in Tiger Moth open-cockpit trainers, and Lee seemed to have natural ability as a pilot. However, on the last training flight before his solo, he was with his instructor pilot at five thousand feet when an intense headache resulted in a loss of vision, forcing him to turn control of the craft over to his instructor. Sent immediately to the medical officer upon landing, he was examined and found to have an "unreliable" optic nerve and grounded. With bad eyes, bombardier and gunner were also eliminated as options, and so Christmas 1941 found Lee in Salisbury with no assignment.

Lee volunteered for Military Intelligence and was seconded to the British South Africa Police Force as a warden at Salisbury Prison, where his duties included guarding prisoners. He was promoted to leading aircraftsman and transferred to Durban, then shipped aboard the *New Amsterdam* to the Suez Canal, where he disembarked and was transported by truck to the Kasfarit Staging Camp in Egypt. Once there, he recalled, his time was divided between drill, boredom, sandstorms, and guard duty. He caught malaria and earned the disfavor of his superior, who, disliking his public school background, assigned him the duty of escorting the Arab "honey-wagons" that serviced the camp's latrines.

Lee was finally assigned to No. 37 and No. 70 Squadrons of the 205 Group, comprised of Wellington bombers that flew from Alexandria dropping propaganda leaflets over the Balkans and German-occupied North Africa encouraging the Germans to surrender. Finally brought before a commissions board, Lee was promoted to pilot officer on 28 January 1943. After a one-week leave, he reported to the 260 Squadron as the new intelligence officer.

The 260 Squadron supported the Army on its advance from El Alamein, west across Libya and into Tunisia. The planes of Lee's unit strafed enemy infantry and bombed any targets requested by the Army. Lee's duties included planning the missions, maintaining communication between the squadron and the Army, and debriefing returning pilots. A large part of the mission's success or failure depended on timely intelligence, which Lee worked hard to provide. Following close behind the advancing Army, Lee came under fire on several occasions, once being strafed by an ME 109 Messerschmitt and receiving a wound to his posterior. On 28 July 1943 he was promoted to flying officer.

Following his transfer from the Middle East to Sicily, information becomes scarce regarding Lee's activities, but it is known that he was involved with Special Forces over a two-year period, which included working with the Special Air Service, Popski's Private Army, and the Special Operations Executive. His unit finished the war with decorations from Czechoslovakia, Yugoslavia, and Poland. He himself was decorated for Distinguished Service. In November 1945 he earned a promotion to flight lieutenant.

Following the war, Lee remained in the military, involved with the war crimes investigations. As part of his duties he visited concentration camps and interrogated civilians and military, including SS officers. It is believed that Lee acquired many of his languages during this period. (He speaks French, Italian, German, and Spanish, and can "get along" in Swedish, Russian, and Greek.) He opted, however, not to follow his father into a military career: "Five years of war, thank you, are enough for most people."

Following his discharge on 17 October 1946, Lee returned to London, where he began taking bit parts in films the following year. He appeared in Laurence Olivier's *Hamlet* in 1948—coincidentally, the first time he would work with fellow actor Peter Cushing.

Lee achieved international fame in 1957 for his portrayal of the Frankenstein creature in *The Curse of Frankenstein*, with Cushing playing Dr. Frankenstein. Lee is reputed to have hated the required makeup, but he nonetheless took the lead the following year in *Dracula* (U.S. title, *Horror of Dracula*, 1958). In all, he portrayed Count Dracula eight times on screen. The ring he wore for his portrayals of the count was a replica of the one worn by Bela Lugosi when he played the king of vampires.

Lee's other memorable films include *The Mummy* (1959), several appearances as Fu Manchu in the 1960s, and three portrayals of Sherlock Holmes. Although he was the first pick of his cousin, Ian Fleming, to play the part of Dr. No in the 1962 film of the same name, the part went to Joseph Wiseman. However, he was successful in securing the role of the villainous Scaramanga in *The Man with the Golden Gun* (1974). He played minor roles in *Julius Caesar* (1970), *The Three Musketeers* (1974), *Airport '77* (1977), and Steven Spielberg's *1941* (1979). More recent work includes *Gremlins II* (1990), Tim Burton's *Sleepy Hollow* (1999), Peter Jacobson's

The Lord of the Rings (2001), and George Lucas's *Star Wars— Episode II* (2002).

Lee has been married for the last forty years to Danish model and painter Gitte Kroencke, with whom he has one daughter, Christina. In 1977, W. H. Allen published his autobiography, *Tall, Dark, and Gruesome,* which was updated in 1997.

Patrick Macnee

Descended from the British aristocracy, Daniel Patrick Macnee was born on 6 February 1922 to a horse-trainer father and socialite mother. His father, Maj. Daniel Macnee, had been an officer in the Yorkshire Dragoons during World War I. Macnee spent his early years at Wiltshire Downs near Marlborough. Raised in a succession of boarding schools, he was taught to show no emotion and was admonished regarding his responsibility to the lower classes. When his father left the family to take a position in India in 1929, Macnee and his mother moved in with a wealthy friend. He was raised with material generosity but a poverty of affection or approval and was shipped off to Eton College at age twelve.

At Eton, Macnee acted in plays and joined the Officers Training Corps (OTC). As such, he was part of the honor guard at the funeral

(Photofest)

Patrick Macnee with his wife Barbara in 1942. Macnee entered the Royal Navy that same year, was commissioned and assigned as navigator to motor torpedo boat (MTB) 415 at Dartmouth. MTB 415 patrolled the English Channel protecting convoys, hunting U-boats, and rescuing downed aircrewmen. He was transferred to MTB 434, which was preparing for the D-Day invasion when Macnee was hospitalized with bronchitis. The boat was sunk in action and two members of the crew received Distinguished Service Crosses. (Patrick Macnee collection)

for King George V at St. George's Chapel in January 1936. He was asked to leave Eton prior to graduation because of improper conduct. With the start of World War II in September 1939, he considered enlisting but decided to wait to be called up. He spent his time performing in plays and smuggling gin. He was in London during the blitz bombings and recalled a wartime London filled with Poles, Czechs, French, Canadians, and Australians. He and the other actors would carouse in the underground shelters after performances. He had just been advised by his agent that he had been selected for a part in the upcoming film *Tuesday's Child* when he received his call-up papers (Stewart Granger took the part).

Macnee entered the Royal Navy on 5 October 1942 as a seaman recruit and took the six-week induction course at a former holiday camp at Pwllheli on the Welsh coast. He took the sea course of basic training aboard HMS *Glendower* and was promoted to able seaman upon its completion. He was sent north, stationed aboard the paddle steamer HMS *Whippingham,* which was used on antiaircraft duty.

He applied for a commission and went before the board, who must have been impressed by Eton and OTC because Macnee was commissioned a sub-lieutenant in the Royal Navy Reserve at Dover, Felixshaw, in June 1943, and sent to HMS *Alfred* outside Brighton for training. He studied engine maintenance, flags, gunnery, Morse code, navigation, radar, signaling, minelaying, and use of torpedoes. After completing the school, he took advanced training courses at Davenport and the Royal Naval College at Greenwich.

Assigned to motor torpedo boats (MTBs), Macnee trained for service with the Light Coastal Forces at Fort William in Scotland, which he recalled as having "the highest rainfall in England." He arrived in Dartmouth in 1943 and was assigned as navigator aboard MTB 415. The boat was 71^1/$_2$ feet long with a beam of 19 feet and a speed of 38–40 knots. It was armed with machine guns, torpedoes, and depth charges. Their mission was to patrol the English Channel protecting convoys and hunting German submarines—and, on one occasion, picking up members of the underground from the Dutch coast. Macnee modestly sums up his wartime services as "not much," but the reality was that he daily risked his life, as did all MTB sailors, patrolling the North Sea. The unpredictable sea was dangerous enough without factoring in enemy aircraft, vessels, torpedoes, and mines.

Prior to the Normandy invasion in June 1944, Macnee was assigned as first lieutenant on MTB 434. He went to Portsmouth to prepare for the invasion but was in the hospital in Chichester with bronchitis on D-Day. MTB 434 was sunk in action on D-Day plus 8, and two of the crew received Distinguished Service Crosses. Macnee questioned the effectiveness of the MTBs and recalled that they did little damage: "They were fast, but weren't good in heavy seas." He also recalled that unlike the German diesel boats (E-boats), they were able to maintain their top speed of 45 knots for only about five minutes.

Macnee was demobilized in 1946 and returned to the stage. He did some minor film work, including parts in *The Elusive Pimpernel* (1950) and *Jane Eyre* (1957), but it was television that made his career. On 9 September 1960 he was offered the part of sidekick to Ian Hendry in the television series *Police Surgeon*. The title was changed to *The Avengers,* and the show made Macnee an international star. The show, which starred Macnee as John Steed, lasted almost a decade (1960–69) and became a cult favorite, no doubt in part thanks to a string of leading ladies that included Diana Rigg, Honor Blackman, Joanna Lumley, and Linda Thorson.

Macnee's subsequent film career runs the spectrum of parts, from films like *Matt Helm* (1975) and *A View to a Kill* (1985) to *This Is Spinal Tap* (1984) and *Lobster Man from Mars* (1990).

Macnee remains active into the twenty-first century, doing television, movies, and theater and narrating books-on-tape. His autobiography, *Blind in One Ear,* was published in 1989, and his memoirs, *The Avengers and Me,* in 1997.

★

Victor McLaglen

Noted as playing men of adventure on the silver screen, Victor McLaglen led a life that rivaled any of his roles in film. He ran away to join the Army, prospected for gold in Australia, wrestled professionally in Canada, boxed professionally in the United States and England, fought in World War I, served as a policeman, and worked in vaudeville and with the circus. And he worked in films with stars like Mae West, Shirley Temple, and John Wayne, winning an Oscar in 1935.

McLaglen was born in Tunbridge Wells, Kent, England, but the exact date of his birth has been reported by various sources as 11 December 1883, 11 December 1886, and 10 December 1886. His memorial at Forest Lawn in Glendale, California, where he is buried, gives 10 December 1886 as his date of birth, as does the *Almanac of Famous People*.

(Photofest)

McLaglen at a World War I ceremony. He enlisted at age fourteen as a private in the Life Guards hoping to see action in the Boer War but was immediately discharged when his age became known. During World War I he enlisted in the Irish Fusiliers of the British army, soldiered in the Middle East, and won an appointment as provost marshal for the city of Baghdad. (Photofest)

He was the oldest of eight sons of the Right Reverend Andrew McLaglen, and five of his brothers—Cyril, Leopold, Clifford, Arthur, and Kenneth—would also go on to work in films. McLaglen moved with his family to Cape Town, South Africa, when his father was appointed bishop of Claremont. His first taste of adventure came when, at age fourteen, he lied about his age and enlisted as a private in the Life Guards, hoping to see combat in the Boer War. He was located by his father, who arranged for his discharge.

In 1904, McLaglen traveled to Canada to work on farms but soon found more lucrative work as a professional wrestler and prizefighter. From 1909 to 1914, he toured with circuses, vaudeville troupes, and wild west shows, traveling across Canada, the United States, and even Australia, where he prospected in the Kalgoorlie gold fields and boxed six rounds against heavyweight champion Jack Johnson. He was home in Cape Town with his family when World War I broke out.

McLaglen returned to England and enlisted in the Irish Fusiliers of the British Army, soldiering in the Middle East, where he rose to the rank of captain and won an appointment as provost marshal for the city of Baghdad. He also boxed while he was in the Army, winning the British Army Heavyweight Championship in 1918.

Leaving the Army, McLaglen returned to boxing in 1919–20 and was working out in the National Sporting Club when he was spotted by producer I. B. Davidson, who offered him the lead in the British silent film *The Call of the Road* (1920). The film and his performance in it were well received, and McLaglen soon found himself being offered roles in other British films like *Carnival* (1921), *Prey of the Dragon* and *The Sport of Kings* (both 1922), *The Romany* (1923), and *Women and Diamonds* (1924).

Summoned to Hollywood in 1924 to play in *The Beloved Brute*, McLaglen had a supporting role in the Ronald Colman version of *Beau Geste* (1926) and a lead in *What Price Glory* (1926), playing Captain Flagg to Edmund Lowe's Sergeant Quirt in director Raoul Walsh's adaptation of the Broadway antiwar play. McLaglen and Lowe reprised their roles as Flagg and Quirt in *The Cockeyed World* (1929) and *Women of All Nations* (1931).

During the next two decades McLaglen would work with some of the greats of twentieth-century cinema: Humphrey Bogart in *A Devil with Women* (1930), Marlene Dietrich in *Dishonored* (1931), Mae West in *Klondike Annie* (1936), Cary Grant and Douglas Fairbanks, Jr., in *Gunga Din* (1939), and Bob Hope and Virginia Mayo in *The Princess and the Pirate* (1944). But it was with director John Ford that McLaglen did some of his best work.

McLaglen had his first speaking role under the direction of Ford in *The Black Watch* (1929), playing opposite Myrna Loy as a British officer in India. In 1934 he worked with Boris Karloff in *The Lost Patrol*, playing the sole survivor of a British patrol in the desert, followed by *The Informer* (1935), in which his performance as the slow-witted Gypo Nolan, an Irish rebel in 1922 Dublin, won him a Best Actor Oscar.

Ford directed McLaglen with Shirley Temple in *Wee Willie Winkie* (1937) and his U.S. Cavalry trilogy: *Fort Apache* (1948), again with Shirley Temple, and *She Wore a Yellow Ribbon* (1949) and *Rio Grande* (1950), both with John Wayne. His last role with Wayne was in Ford's *The Quiet Man* (1952), for which he was nominated for a Best Supporting Actor Oscar, playing Maureen O'Hara's brother.

Shortly after being directed by his son, Andrew V. McLaglen, in *The Abductors* (1957), McLaglen suffered a heart attack and died in Newport Beach, California, on 7 November 1959.

Toshiro Mifune

I f, as it is said, sword-wielding samurai epics are the Japanese
equivalent of the American western, then it is fair to say that
Toshiro Mifune is Japan's John Wayne. Just as John Wayne sym-
bolized the qualities of character valued by Americans, Mifune repre-
sented the *tateyaku* (heroic leading man) tradition of Japan, portraying the Japanese ideal of manliness in characters who are brave,
strong-willed, ascetic, and self-sacrificing.

His long collaboration with legendary director Akira Kurosawa created a Japanese cinema that was admired and often imitated by Hollywood. In seventeen years (1948–65), Mifune starred in sixteen Kuro-
sawa-directed films, which included some of his best work: *Rashomon*
(Into the Woods, 1950), his masterpiece *Seven Samurai* (1954), and
Yojimbo (The Bodyguard, 1961). His appearance in more than 130

(Photofest)

films, both Japanese and American, earned him international fame and a place as one of the great figures of twentieth-century cinema.

Toshiro Mifune was born in Quingdao (Tsingtao), China, to Japanese parents, Tokuzo and Sen Mifune, in what was then Japanese-occupied Manchuria on 1 April 1920. His parents were Methodist missionaries, and Mifune was raised in that faith. He grew up in China, helping occasionally in his father's photo lab, and graduated from Port Arthur High School. When the Sino-Japanese War broke out, after an exchange of gunfire across the Marco Polo Bridge, Mifune's family returned to Japan. Back home, he studied photography before being called up for military service shortly after his twentieth birthday in 1940.

Conscripted into the Imperial Army Air Force, Mifune studied aerial photography at an Air Force training facility in Manchuria. He recalled in an interview years later that he was anxious about the killing that lay ahead and reluctant to leave his family, whom he feared he might never see again (and indeed, both parents died during the war). He remembered the hardships and the "blood lust" that his training stirred in him.

During the war, Mifune went on flying missions learning the craft of aerial photography, so vital to intelligence in the developing air war between the Allies and the Axis powers. One source mentions that among his other duties, Mifune was responsible for serving the ceremonial sake to departing kamikaze pilots.

Following the Japanese surrender on 2 September 1945, Mifune was discharged from the defeated Japanese Army Air Force at Kyushu, Japan. Born and raised in Manchuria, he had no real home. Without family or friends, he decided to remain in Japan, moving in with an Army buddy in Tokyo. There were few jobs in occupied Japan, especially for aspiring photographers, and he unsuccessfully went from job to job until he heard of an opening for an assistant cameraman from another Army buddy in the spring of 1946.

Mifune's application to the Toho Film Company, the largest studio in Japan, changed his life. In an attempt to improve box office receipts, the studio had launched a massive "new faces" contest, soliciting applications from would-be actors all across the country. Mifune's application for the cameraman's position had become mixed in with more than four thousand applicants for actors, and he was called in for an interview. Auditioning reluctantly, he came to the attention of director Kajiro Yamamoto, who was impressed with Mifune's innate talent and recommended him to another director, Senkichi Taniguchi, who cast him in his first role, a small part in *Shin Baka Jidai* (These Foolish Times, 1947). Also witnessing the screen test was a third director, Akira Kurosawa.

Mifune's first film for Kurosawa was the 1948 movie *Yoidore Tenshi* (Drunken Angel), in which he played a young hoodlum with tuberculosis living in a Tokyo slum. His performance was so overpowering that Kurosawa altered the script of the film to make Mifune's character more central to the story line. Kurosawa recalled, "This was the first picture in which my original idea was turned upside-down." Four of the next five films Mifune made were with Kurosawa: *Quiet Duel* and *Stray Dog* in 1949, and *Scandal* and *Rashomon* in 1950.

Often called Kurosawa's first great film, *Rashomon,* set in feudal Japan, relates the story of the murder of a nobleman and the rape of his wife told from the widely differing perspectives of four characters; the wife, the ghost of the nobleman, the woodcutter who witnessed the incidents, and the bandit who committed them. Mifune played the bandit, Matsunaga, to glowing reviews. The film won the Grand Prize at the Venice International Film Festival in 1951, as well as an Academy Award for Best Foreign Language Film later that year.

Other films with Kurosawa followed, including *Hakuchi* (1951), an adaptation of Fyodor Dostoevsky's masterpiece, *The Idiot; Kumonosu Jo* (Throne of Blood, 1957), Shakespeare's *Macbeth* transported to medieval Japan; and *Yojimbo* (1961), for which Mifune won his first of two Best Actor Awards at the Venice Film Festival; the other was *Akaige* (Red Beard, 1965), his last film with Kurosawa.

Mifune's first American film appearance was in *Grand Prix* (1966), for which the actor learned English. Although he made many fine American films, his performances lacked the power he projected in Japanese films, since American movie producers felt that his dynamic acting style had to be toned down in order to appeal to Western audiences. His notable American films include *Hell in the Pacific* (1968), with Lee Marvin; *Red Sun* (1971), with Alain Delon and Charles Bronson; *Paper Tiger* (1975), with David Niven; and *Midway* (1976), in which he played Japan's Adm. Isoroku Yamamoto. He had previously portrayed the admiral in two other films, *Storm over the Pacific* (1960) and *Admiral Yamamoto* (1968).

Perhaps the role for which he is best remembered was that of Lord Toranaga in the 1980 television mini-series *Shogun,* based on James Clavell's novel of the same name. The series, which starred Richard Chamberlain, won a Limited Series Emmy.

Mifune continued to work in the industry until his last film, *Fukai Kawa* (Deep River, 1995). He became ill following the completion of the movie and died at his home in Tokyo on 24 December 1997, at the age of seventy-seven.

Roger Moore

The man who replaced Sean Connery as Agent 007 on the big screen, Roger Moore has appeared in seven films portraying Ian Fleming's legendary British secret agent, James Bond: *Live and Let Die* (1973), *The Man with the Golden Gun* (1974), *The Spy Who Loved Me* (1977), *Moonraker* (1979), *For Your Eyes Only* (1981), *Octopussy* (1983), and *A View to a Kill* (1985).

The son of a policeman, Roger George Moore was born in Stockwell, London, on 14 October 1927. He was twelve at the outbreak of World War II and grew up in an England at war, with blitz bombs, rationing, and the spirit of national unity all part of his adolescence. He volunteered for national service in the autumn of 1945, at the end of the war.

Following six weeks of basic training at Bury St. Edwards, Private Moore, a trained and talented graphic artist, was put to work draw-

(Photofest)

Moore volunteered for national service at the end of World War II. He was commissioned as a second lieutenant in 1946, at the age of nineteen, and posted to Schleswig-Holstein, West Germany, as a member of the occupying force. Moore was later assigned to the Combined Services Entertainment Unit, and was demobilized in 1948. (Roger Moore collection)

ing posters for the Army before being accepted for officer training. He underwent officer candidate training, then took additional field training with a motor transport company at Dartford (Kent) and in North Wales. In 1946, at the age of nineteen, he was commissioned a second lieutenant.

Posted overseas to Schleswig-Holstein in (then) West Germany with the army of occupation, Lieutenant Moore was assigned to command a small supply depot. His easygoing manner resulted in good commander/unit relations, if not always good military order and discipline. Later transferred to a larger depot, where he was second in command and discipline more "traditional," Moore requested transfer to the Combined Services Entertainment Unit (CSEU), a military entertainment command similar to the American Special Services. He was not accepted.

Back in his unit, a jeep accident resulted in an emergency appendectomy and a seven-week stay in a military hospital in Hamburg. After a leave at the end of 1946, during which he married Doorn Van Steyn, he returned to Germany and was posted to Lippstaadt as welfare officer with No. 4 Training Brigade.

Finally accepted to the CSEU in Hamburg, Moore was promoted to first lieutenant and acting captain by the War Office Selection Board. Because he was an officer, he was permitted only to produce, not to perform. Unlike the civilian-run Entertainments National Service Association (ENSA), the CSEU was a military unit, tasked with producing and arranging all types of entertainment (shows, plays, concerts, etc.), and Moore oversaw productions of *Charley's Aunt* and *The Hasty Heart* as well as being responsible for the travel arrangements of visiting performers like Spike Milligan and Kay Kendall. During this time, in September 1947, he also auditioned for a part in *Blue Lagoon* (1949) with Jean Simmons. He was unsuccessful, as was Laurence Harvey, who also lost out to Donald Houston.

Moore returned to headquarters in Hamburg, where he was demobilized in the spring of 1948. After studying at the Royal Academy of Dramatic Arts, he came to the United States in 1952, finding work just two weeks after arriving, in the appropriately titled television play *World by the Tail*. Work in films such as *The Last Time I Saw Paris* (1954) and *The King's Thief* (1955) gave way to work in television series such as *Ivanhoe* (1958), *The Alaskans* (1959–60), *Maverick* (1960–61), and *The Saint* (1967–69).

Moore returned to the big screen with the Bond movies and other films like *Shout at the Devil* (1978), *The Wild Geese* (1979), *North Sea Hijack* (also released as *ffolkes* and *Assault Force,* 1979), *Sunday Lovers* (1981), and *Cannonball Run* (1985). One of the world's most recognizable faces, he has never lacked for work, but recently he has preferred roles as a narrator in films or television productions to appearances in film.

Moore has been married twice since his divorce from Doorn Van Steyn, to singer Dorothy Squires (1953–69) and Italian former starlet Luisa Mattioli (1969–96).

★

Kenneth More

Born into a solidly middle-class family in Gerrard's Cross, England, on 20 September 1914, Kenneth Gilbert More was the son
of Gilbert More, a Royal Navy lieutenant and pilot in the Naval
Air Service during World War I.

His father's early death forced More to abandon his dream of studying civil engineering in order to go to work to help support the family. He took work first as a fur trapper and then as an engineering assistant, but eventually a family friend helped him get a job as a stagehand
at London's Windmill Theatre, a burlesque house. Soon More was
appearing onstage doing comedy skits between the nude acts that were
the primary draw, and he realized that he enjoyed performing, which
led to a search for work on a more legitimate stage.

By the mid-1930s More had appeared in his first film, *Look Up and*

Laugh (1935), with Vivien Leigh, followed by *Windmill Revels* and *Carry on London* (both 1938). He was working as an actor in Wolverhampton when war broke out in September 1939, and he promptly went to enlist in the Royal Navy, hoping to follow in his father's footsteps.

At the recruiting station More was brusquely told that they had sufficient men at present, and he was instructed to return home to await being called up. Instead, seeing a notice for Air Raid Precautions, he signed up as an air raid warden. During the period of the "phony" war (1939–40), More had his fill of rolling bandages and tending imaginary victims of imaginary air raids, so in the spring of 1940, when he was invited to join the Defensively Equipped Merchant Ships (DEMS), he was ready for a change and readily volunteered.

Because of the threat to shipping posed by German U-boats, the DEMS merchant ships were fitted with guns, and a naval gunnery rating was assigned to each gun, with a gun team drawn from the crew. Within a few weeks Ordinary Seaman More was ordered to Portsmouth, to report to HMS *Victory* for basic naval training, followed by training in the care and operation of 4-inch guns at Tiger Bar, Cardiff.

In May 1940, upon completing his training, Able Seaman More was assigned to the cargo ship MV *Lobos,* a merchantman of the Pacific Steam Navigation Company bound for the west coast of South America. The trip would take the convoy through the southern Irish Sea, an area heavily patrolled by German U-boats. They boarded the *Lobos* in Liverpool, and the cruise was uneventful until their escort left them at the southern end of the Irish Sea. That night the tanker *Athelaird* was lost to a torpedo in a spectacular explosion, and More became painfully aware of the vulnerability of their slow-moving ships to the weapons of the swifter U-boats.

They traveled from Bermuda to Cuba and through the Panama Canal, making stops along the American coast. They stopped in Talcahuano, in neutral Chile, for repairs that took nine weeks. More was less than thrilled at having to spend the additional time in Chile, which although officially neutral was decidedly pro-German. Finally they docked at Valparaíso.

On the return trip, loaded with iron ore and bat guano, the *Lobos* joined up with HX 84 in the Caribbean, bound for Halifax. On 5 November the convoy was attacked by the German pocket-battleship *Admiral Scheer,* with the resulting loss of five ships, including the armed merchant cruiser *Jervis Bay.*

Returning to Portsmouth, More learned that his application for a commission had been approved, and in early January 1941 he was sent to Lancing College in Sussex for five weeks of training, then to HMS *King Alfred.* He emerged as Temporary Acting Sub-Lieutenant Kenneth More, RNVR (Royal Navy Volunteer Reserve). Having hoped for an assignment to the fleet, More was dismayed to discover that he was being reassigned to the Merchant Navy, his experience being deemed too valuable to pass up, and he was assigned to teach antiaircraft gunnery to Merchant Navy officers. He immediately applied to the Admiralty for reassignment, but without success. Finally a petty officer confided that a surefire way to get reassigned was to become ill. More feigned appendicitis so successfully that he was hospitalized at Blundell Sands and had his perfectly good appendix removed. He was also successful in his goal of being reassigned, and while on medical leave he applied for a gunnery course at Whale Island, off Portsmouth, anticipating assignment to a ship following graduation.

Finally, in May 1942, More was ordered to Liverpool and assigned to HMS *Aurora,* a light cruiser, as a high-angle gunnery officer. He was also promoted to full lieutenant. The ship sailed north on 4 July, escorting minelayers whose aim was to block U-boats from sneaking into the Atlantic from the North Sea. More recalled feeling more in danger from icebergs than from enemy subs.

From the frigid reaches of the North Sea the *Aurora* next sailed south, escorting a convoy transporting Scottish troops to reinforce Gen. Bernard Montgomery in North Africa. The *Aurora* escorted the convoy as far as Freetown, in Sierra Leone, then after a two-week stay returned to the Mediterranean in November 1942 in support of Operation Torch, the invasion of North Africa.

Lieutenant More was control officer, in command of the *Aurora*'s 4-inch antiaircraft guns, when they began to patrol the waters off Oran, Algeria, with the mission of preventing the escape of any French warships from the harbor. In an interview in the November 1977 issue of *After the Battle,* More recalled, "We didn't want to fight the French, but we had our orders." The prospect that the French warships might be added to the German and Italian navies prompted the British to take drastic action. British officials decided that the French warships anchored at Oran had to be either destroyed or disabled. On 3 June 1940, British Marines boarded all French ships anchored at Plymouth and Portsmouth and put their crews ashore. On that same day, British Naval Force H appeared off Oran. The French naval squadron there was given several options. Its commanders could join forces with the British; sail to a British port; sail to a French port in the West Indies; or sail to the United States, disarmed. Adm. Marcel Gensould, who commanded the French naval forces, refused the options offered by the British and cleared his ships for action. The British quickly went into action, sinking one French battleship, setting another on fire, and severely damaging the battle cruiser *Dunkerque*. Thirteen hundred French sailors were lost. A few French warships escaped to Toulon, but the French Navy had ceased to exist.

The next morning a French destroyer attempted to run the blockade, and after a twenty-minute exchange of fire, the French destroyer was on fire and intentionally run aground by her captain, while the *Aurora* suffered no damage. At 1100 hours two more French destroyers made a run for it. Assisted by the British destroyer *Boadicea,* the smaller of the two French destroyers was knocked out of action, and the larger withdrew, ending the naval resistance by the French.

The *Aurora* was next assigned as the flagship of Rear Adm. Sir Cecil Harcourt's 12th Cruiser Squadron, Force Q, which consisted of the *Aurora,* two other cruisers, the *Sirius* and *Argonaut,* and two destroyers, the *Quiberon* and *Quentin*. Force Q's mission was to disrupt Rommel's supply lines, breaking the link between Sicily and Tripoli.

On the night of 1–2 December the task force clashed with two German destroyers escorting four merchant ships, and six ships were sent to the bottom. German dive bombers made regular appearances, and the captain became aware that morale was suffering among the crewmen below decks, who were unaware of the progress of the battle. So because of More's experience as a performer—or perhaps, as he suspected, because of his inaccuracy as a gunnery officer—he was taken off the antiaircraft guns and stationed on the lower bridge with a microphone connected to a loudspeaker, from where he gave a play-

More signing autographs during filming of *Reach for the Sky* (1956), the true story of Wing Commander Douglas Bader, an RAF pilot with prosthetic legs who flew during the Battle of Britain. Bader had lost his legs when he was shot down over German-held territory. During his captivity, the Germans allowed the RAF to paradrop him a new pair of prostheses. (Photofest)

by-play of the battle for the crew. This proved so popular that the idea was copied by other ships in the fleet.

The *Aurora* remained in the area of operations through the winter of 1942 and into the summer of 1943. On 7 June 1943 the ship served as an observation platform for Adm. Sir Andrew Cunningham and Gen. Dwight Eisenhower, who were on board to view the bombardment of Pantelleria, an Italian naval base, and it later transported King George VI from Tripoli to Malta.

The *Aurora* was next involved in operations during the invasion of Sicily, bombarding the mainland prior to the invasion. The *Aurora* fired on Catania, in Sicily, at 0115 hours on 10 July 1943, earning the distinction of firing the first shots of the Allies returning to mainland Europe, then forced the Straits of Messina.

Following an engagement off Salerno in which the *Aurora* fired on and destroyed seven armored cars on shore, the ship went into dry dock at Malta until 4 October, when it transported troops to the islands of Cos and Leros in the Aegean Sea, risking attack by German bombers stationed on the island of Rhodes. They traversed the gauntlet twice more without serious incident, but on their fourth crossing on 30 October 1943 they were less fortunate, and the ship was attacked by a flight of Junker 87 dive bombers escorted by Messerschmitt fighters.

A near miss nearly did More in when fragments from an exploding bomb wounded a man beside him, a newsreel cameraman named Hardy. Ammunition began exploding, and the stern was severely damaged, with a loss of forty-three men. More thought it was the end when another flight of dive bombers approached, but the enemy fortunately went after the *Aurora*'s destroyer-escorts. The memory of the carnage that night remained with More for the rest of his life.

As the *Aurora* made its way back to Alexandria, burying its dead on the way, More reflected on the irony of his having been moved from gunner to ship's broadcaster. The individual who had replaced More at the gunnery station had been killed while More, who was on the lower bridge broadcasting, came through unscathed.

Following the armistice with Italy, the *Aurora* sailed to Taranto, the Italian naval base, for a major overhaul.

By Christmas 1944, after over two years aboard the *Aurora,* More was ready to move on, so he volunteered for training as a fire direction officer. Accepted, he returned to England and was sent to Yeovilton, Somerset, for two months of training, graduating second in his class. Following leave, he was assigned to HMS *Victorious,* an aircraft carrier in the Pacific, and was en route to the Pacific aboard the troopship *New Amsterdam* in the Red Sea on VE-Day. After three weeks in Sydney, Australia, he reported aboard the *Victorious* as second flight director officer and was involved in continuous bombing operations against the Japanese mainland until the end of the war.

Following his discharge, More returned to the theater, appearing both in the West End of London and in regional repertory theaters. His first postwar film, *Scott of the Antarctic* (1948), was followed by several others, including *Man on the Run* and *Stop Press Girl* (both

1949), *The Franchise Affair* (1950), *Appointment with Venus* (1951), and *Brandy for the Parson* (1952). But it was with a pair of comedies that More gained star status. He was nominated for the British Academy of Film and Television Arts (BAFTA) Best Actor award for the film *Genevieve* (1953), an award he won the following year for *Doctor in the House* (1954). His string of successes continued with a Best Actor win at the Venice Film Festival in 1955 for *The Deep Blue Sea,* a film for which he was also nominated for a BAFTA Best Actor award, and another BAFTA Best Actor nomination the following year for *Reach for the Sky* (1956).

By the end of the 1950s, cinematic audiences were changing, and although he began working more on television, More continued to make films, some memorable—*A Night to Remember* (1958), Hitchcock's *The Thirty-nine Steps* (1959), *Sink the Bismarck* (1960), *The Longest Day* (1962), and *Battle of Britain* (1969)—and some not so memorable, such as *The Sheriff of Fractured Jaw* (1958), with Jayne Mansfield, and Disney's *Unidentified Flying Oddball* (1979), his last film appearance.

More wrote two autobiographies, *Happy-Go-Lucky* (1959) and *More of Less* (1978). He died of Parkinson's disease in London on 12 July 1982.

★

David Niven

V oted the Best Motion Picture of 1956 by the Academy of Motion Picture Arts and Sciences and the New York Film Critics, the movie version of Jules Verne's *Around the World in Eighty Days* was a gigantic color production in which some thirty major stars appeared. The lead actor was Scottish-born David Niven, a dapper, suave émigré who had come to Hollywood in 1935 and established himself as one of the industry's finest character actors, appearing in over sixty movies. A wavy-haired charmer with a pencil-thin mustache, Niven is remembered for superb performances in movies such as *Wuthering Heights* (1939), with Laurence Olivier and Merle Oberon; *The Bishop's Wife* (1948), with Cary Grant and Loretta Young; *The Moon Is Blue* (1954), with William Holden and Maggie McNamara; and *The Guns of Navarone* (1961), with Gregory Peck and Anthony Quinn. Niven's presence has added a unique flavor to many other movies as well, including the popular Pink Panther series. His portrayal of a fraudulent major in *Separate Tables* (1958), with Deborah Kerr and Rita Hayworth, won him a Best Actor Academy Award.

Niven was born in 1910 in Kirriemuir, Scotland. Some of his earliest memories included witnessing the German Zeppelin raids on London in 1915. His father, Lt. William Edward Graham Niven, was in the Berkshire Yeomanry of the Territorial Army and was killed in 1915 during the disastrous World War I campaign at Gallipoli, Turkey. In this effort, British and French forces attempted to open the Dardanelles to supply arms to Russia's immense manpower reserve. Nearly half a million British, Australian and New Zealand Army Corps (ANZAC), and French soldiers were landed on the beaches of Gallipoli, where Turkish forces opposed them in fierce fighting. Gaining little ground, the invasion soon became stalemated, and the battle bogged down into trench warfare. Each side suffered enormous losses. Before they withdrew, British, ANZAC, and French units had suffered 250,000 casualties. Because of this fiasco, Winston Churchill was forced out as first lord of the Admiralty, his sterling reputation tarnished and not restored until World War II.

Niven was an unruly schoolboy. Concerned, and anxious for some proper discipline for the boy, his mother hoped to get him enrolled as an officer cadet at the prestigious Royal Naval Academy at Dartmouth. At the time, boys entered the college at age thirteen and a half, graduating as naval officers four years later. But the sea service would not be in Niven's future; after two days of testing, he failed the entrance examinations.

While attending Stowe School in Buckinghamshire, a British public school, however, he was able to pass the entrance exam to the Royal Military College at Sandhurst, the British equivalent of West Point. After ten weeks of basic drilling and ceremonies, which British servicemen call "square bashing," Niven was promoted to lance corporal and assigned to be the commandant's orderly for six months. Later his company was designated Champion Drill Company, and he was authorized to wear a prestigious red lanyard—that is, a cord that members of a decorated unit wear around the left shoulder. While at Sandhurst, Niven's curriculum consisted of military law, tactics, organization, administration, and riding.

In 1928 he was commissioned a second lieutenant in the Highland Light Infantry (City of Glasgow Regiment), and at the age of eighteen he was sent to his unit at Malta. The young lieutenant would have preferred a commission in the Argyll and Sutherland Highlanders, but the Highland Light was a respected regiment. Raised in 1777, it had earned its first battle honors in the American War of Independence. During World War I, seven Victoria Crosses were awarded to its members.

At the time the young officer was stationed there, Malta was home port of the British Mediterranean Fleet. The day after he arrived, Niven, platoon leader of C Company, in Floriana Barracks, encountered the only action he would see during the doldrums of duty between wars. Ordered to protect a customs house in Valletta harbor, his platoon encountered local hooligans armed with iron bars and stones. However, when faced with one of Niven's fierce Scottish troopers, the troublemakers soon retreated.

The next four years were characterized by daily training, though one good anecdote did emerge: Niven had been ordered to advance his platoon over a mile and a half of open ground. The colonel observing the exercise had authorized him to use a road through the area. But once out of the colonel's sight, Lieutenant Niven put his platoon on a local bus that delivered them to a location behind the colonel. Leaving the bus, Niven and his men snuck to the rear of the colonel's position and charged, Niven yelling at his superior, "Bang, bang, you're dead!"

In 1932 the battalion was posted back to Great Britain and assigned to Citadel Barracks, Dover. While Niven was stationed there, his French grandmother died, leaving him £200 in her will. He invested half of the money in a secondhand Morris Cowley sports car and joined the London social scene, soon finding himself on the Mayfair hostesses' list. There followed invitations to debutante parties and weekends at country estates. It was at one of these parties that Niven met and danced with future American socialite/heiress Barbara Hutton, who was in London on a short visit. Before she left she made him promise to come to New York for Christmas. He accepted the invitation, to be polite, but forgot about it as he went about his military duties and social activities.

Shortly before Christmas his mother died suddenly, and he felt he had to get away to cope with his grief. He had four weeks' leave on the books, and while trying to decide where he would go he remembered Barbara Hutton's invitation. He cabled her that he was coming to New York, and she cabled back, "Come at once, Love, Barbara." She met him with open arms as he got off the boat in New York. During his stay in the city he was wined and dined by Hutton at parties, speakeasies (Prohibition was the law in America then), and nightclubs. He was introduced to stage and screen celebrities, politicians, and wealthy businessmen and their families. It was a joyous holiday for Niven, and when he returned to the Citadel Barracks, he knew that someday he would return to America.

During his earlier social whirl he had met aspiring actress Ann Todd. By the time he returned from America, her career had taken off, and as he renewed their friendship, he began to get a little stagestruck. She introduced him to various actors and actresses, including a strikingly handsome young man, Laurence Olivier.

The London theater scene quickly became much more exciting than the dull routine of a peacetime Army. Things came to a head during a lecture in a machine-gun course. When the instructor asked if there were any questions, Niven replied, "Could you tell me the time please, I have to catch a train." He resigned from the Army and sailed for Canada the next morning.

Over the next three years, Niven worked as a road builder at a lumber camp in Canada, became a beachcomber in Bermuda, and reportedly trained insurgents in machine gunnery in Cuba. He finally found his way to California in 1935, and though it was difficult to find work in depression-era America, he was hired as a wine salesman in Santa Barbara. One morning he found HMS *Norfolk* at anchor in the bay. That evening he attended a party on board the ship, where he enjoyed himself so much that he passed out. Coming to the next morning, David Niven found himself at sea. But all was well: as a publicity stunt, the *Norfolk* was to meet the MGM prop ship *Metha Nelson,* which had been used as HMS *Bounty* in the hit movie *Mutiny on the Bounty.* Niven transferred to the *Bounty* and found his way home. He would later refer to himself as "the first man to crash Hollywood in a battleship."

During Niven's California sojourn, Hollywood director Edmund Goulding agreed to give him a screen test. Afterward, they discussed a two-year contract. But around this same time Niven's visa ran out, and the immigration authorities gave him twenty-four hours to leave

Niven with his wife, Primula Rollo, at their wedding in 1940. (Photofest)

the country. Accordingly, he went to Mexico and waited to be granted a resident alien's permit. He reentered the United States later that same year. In the meantime, his screen test had been accepted, and he was classified in the studios as Anglo Saxon Type No. 2008. The first part the Anglo got was as a Mexican in a Hopalong Cassidy film. He appeared in twenty-seven westerns as a walk-on or extra before MGM offered him a seven-year contract. Four years after that, David Niven was a major Hollywood star.

Then, on 3 September 1939, his native country declared war on Germany. Niven went back to join Britain's military forces. Returning via Italy (not yet in the war), he twice played golf with Mussolini's brother-in-law, Count Ciano, continuing on to Paris and then London. Because of his role in *The First of the Few* (1942), a movie about Spitfire designer Reginald Mitchell, Niven wanted to join the Royal Air Force (RAF). But the RAF at the time pointedly did not want actors, and Niven was turned down. Although he was becoming recognized by moviegoers because of his appearances in American films, the British press criticized him for not being in uniform.

Niven was frequently invited to exclusive parties and dinners. On one occasion during a formal dinner in February 1940, Winston Churchill, by this time prime minister, rose and walked over to him. Shaking hands with the embarrassed actor, Churchill commented, "Young man, you did a very fine thing to give up a most promising career and return to fight for your country. Mind you, had you not done so it would have been despicable!"

In the end, it was a chance meeting on the balcony of a London nightclub that saved Niven from further embarrassment. Lt. Col. Jimmy Boswell, commander of the 2nd Battalion of the Rifle Brigade, asked if he would join their ranks. The Rifle Brigade based at Tidworth, often referred to as "the Prince Consort's Own," was a unit whose history went back to the Napoleonic Wars. Deeply honored, Niven fretted that the antics of his early military career would hurt his chances now. But he worried for naught; he was ordered to report to the brigade as a lieutenant.

The 2nd Battalion was a motor training battalion, and Niven was tasked with the boring job of teaching young men to march and drive trucks. He later trained with the brigade in France, where he served until after the evacuation of Dunkirk. Niven had soon had enough of this brigade, and he volunteered for duty with a new secretive organization that turned out to be Britain's elite commando force. His new, more exciting function involved training in the West Highlands, where he ran up and down mountains, crawled along streams at night, and swam in the loch with full equipment. Upon completion of this tour, he was promoted to captain.

By this time the German blitz of London was in full force. There was a very real possibility that the country could be overrun, and the commando mission prepared to go from offensive to defensive, leading an underground movement. Niven was assigned as liaison officer between the commando units and MO9, the War Office Department that was responsible for them and their operations.

One weekend while on leave at Ditchley, Niven again encountered Winston Churchill. As they walked together, he filled the prime minister in on the commandos' activities. Niven became quite animated and inspired, but Churchill chided him, "Your security is very lax, you should not be telling me this." Churchill was known as a natural actor, but Niven never would discover whether or not he was kidding.

The commandos were now being trained for offensive operations. However, their missions could not begin until suitable landing craft could be built. At the same time, the buildup of a German invasion force on the other side of the channel caused increasing concern. A separate outfit was formed within the Special Forces to deal with this potential danger, and Niven was sent to Richmond, England, to join the unit. Richmond was the headquarters for Phantom reconnaissance squadrons, mobile patrols equipped with communications equipment. Placed among front-line units, they were charged with sending intelligence reports back to force commanders needing clarification of battle situations in order to make quick decisions. After yet more training, Niven was promoted to major. He then commanded Squadron A for three years.

In August 1942 an amphibious assault was made on the French port city of Dieppe. Six thousand commandos—five thousand Canadians and one thousand British—and a small contingent of U.S. Rangers, plus a Phantom team, stormed ashore in landing craft supported by tanks. The Germans were ready for the Allied invaders: they killed, wounded, or captured more than half of the six thousand, and all seven battalion commanders were among the casualties. Though many lessons were learned that would later be applied at Normandy, the cost of this operation was appalling. More sophisticated amphibious equipment would be needed to successfully carry out future such assaults. Dieppe proved the impossibility of capturing port facilities as initial objects of a continental invasion.

As Niven tackled the onerous task of writing letters to the wives and girlfriends of those lost in the battle, A Company began preparing for the coming invasion of Europe. American troops had been pouring into Britain in great numbers, and one morning Niven was ordered to report to Gen. Sir Frederick Morgan, near Sunningdale. General Morgan ordered Niven out of Phantom, promoted him to lieutenant colonel, and placed him under the direct orders of the U.S. Army's Gen. Ray Barker. He was to be liaison officer to General Barker, to ensure that there would be no misunderstandings between the British and American forces during the European invasion.

Before Niven assumed his new responsibilities, he was sent on temporary duty to star in a government-backed patriotic movie, *The Way Ahead*, written by his batman, Peter Ustinov. (Batmen were soldiers assigned to British officers as servants. For details, see Ustinov's chapter.)

Shortly after the D-Day invasion, Niven departed for Normandy on board the American-built merchant ship *Empire Battleaxe*. As the vessel started its journey, Niven watched hundreds of wounded being offloaded from a tank landing craft. With this grim spectacle still in his mind, he spent his first night lying in a ditch in Normandy, listening to the noisy nightingales. In fact, he later said, the birds' racket all but drowned out the sound of gunfire on the beach. In the morning Niven made his way to a small bridge at Carentan. On one side was the British Second Army, on the other the American First. The bridge was a vital link between the meager beachheads the Allies had established, so naturally the Germans shelled it continuously at close range. Niven had to cross it several times to liaise between the two armies, and he spent hours in foxholes on both sides, waiting for German barrages to end. As battles raged around Caen and Saint-Lô longer than had been anticipated, frustrated Allied commanders began squabbling. Finally, by the end of July, the Canadians succeeded in containing most of the German armor. This allowed the Americans to break out on the western flank and head for Paris and Brussels.

Just before the breakout at Falaise, General Barker ordered Niven back to England for a one-on-one briefing on the Allies' front-line movement. By the time he returned to France, the German Seventh Army had been all but wiped out, and the Allied forces were in full pursuit of their retreating enemy. Disputes now arose between the generals, with their various plans to bring the war to an end quickly. Fingers were pointed in an effort to fix blame for the sixteen out of twenty German generals of the Seventh Army who continued to evade capture. Generals Mont-

Commissioned in 1928 as a second lieutenant in the Highland Light Infantry (City of Glasgow Regiment), Niven served during World War II as a lieutenant in the rifle brigade at Tideworth and later with Britain's elite commando force. (Photofest)

gomery, Bradley, and Patton disagreed with each other's plans for what lay ahead, and General Barker and his department had a lot of fence-mending to do. The ever-diplomatic David Niven was a lead negotiator in resolving some of the most contentious issues.

In December 1944 he was at Spa, the American First Army headquarters in the Ardennes, when the Sixth German Panzer Army made its thrust westward. Lt. Col. Otto Skorzeny's Trojan Horse Brigade—speaking English, wearing American uniforms, and using American tanks and half-tracks—infiltrated Allied lines and caused utter confusion. They directed American units at crossroads away from attacking German forces, and they sabotaged Allied ammo and supply dumps as they raced for Meuse. Niven was caught in the middle of the offensive, and nervous GIs stopped him repeatedly, since he was in a British uniform being transported in a U.S. Army jeep. Luckily, because of his movies, he was recognized. Things got iffy on one occasion when he was asked who had won the World Series in 1940. The Scottish-born Niven didn't have the faintest idea, but he tried to establish his credentials by telling the Americans he had made a movie with Ginger Rogers in 1938. They let him pass.

By the end of February 1945, the British Army was fighting fierce battles in the Reichwald. Allied forces were making progress at the Roer and the Maas. By March the American Army had reached the Rhine at Cologne, and the U.S. Third Army was at the junction of the Moselle. The 9th Armored Division crossed the Remagen bridge, securing the first small Allied bridgehead across the Rhine.

In April 1945, Niven crossed the Rhine at Wesel, where he witnessed the town's complete annihilation. Münster had been reduced to the same smoking desolation. Traveling between Hanover and Osnabrück, he passed a huge prisoner-of-war cage holding over one hundred thousand Germans. On a railroad siding near Liebenau, he came across a freight train loaded with V-2 rockets that had surely been destined for London. In a nearby woods he saw the slave labor camp that had manufactured the rockets. Gaunt, bewildered men— Italian, French, Czech, Polish, Dutch, Yugoslav, Russian, Ukrainian— wandered about in a daze, asking how to get home. By 8 May 1945, the war in Europe was over.

The prisoners wondering how to go home were not alone: the routes leading out of Germany to the west were clogged with eight million displaced persons trying to get home. Traveling down a country road one day, Niven and his driver passed through a small village. On the outskirts they met a farm wagon headed for the village. The two men in it wore typical farmers' clothing, but after they had driven on, Niven suddenly realized that one of the farmers had been wearing field boots. He had the driver turn around and stop the wagon.

Niven pulled out his revolver, gesturing to the men to raise their hands. He asked the man with the boots who he was. Dejected, the German general gave his name and rank. Niven asked where he was coming from. "Berlin," the man replied. When asked where he was headed, he said, "Home, it's not far now, only one kilometer." The two stared at each other for some time. The man showed such weariness and blank despair that in the end Niven said, "Go ahead sir, and cover up your bloody boots." The German did as he was told. Then, with a sob that pained Niven to hear, the general covered his face with his hands, and the wagon drove on.

In Britain after the war, General Barker pinned the American Legion of Merit medal on Niven. The British government gave him his demobilization wardrobe: one worsted gray suit, one brown Homburg hat, two poplin shirts with collars, one striped tie, one pair of black shoes, and his freedom. Niven cabled Samuel Goldwyn in Hollywood that he was available for work.

For the next four decades David Niven appeared in numerous films in both Hollywood and Britain. He also worked frequently on television. He was co-founder of the Four Star Production Company, and he starred in *The David Niven Show* (1959) and the series *The Rogues* (1964–65). A year before his death in 1983, he acted in three movies: *Trail of the Pink Panther, Better Late Than Never,* and *Curse of the Pink Panther.*

During World War II Niven married the former Miss Primula ("Primmie") Rollo, an officer in the British Women's Auxiliary Air Force. Tragically, she died in a home accident in 1946 when the family moved to Los Angeles after the war. They had two sons. Two years after her death, Niven married the former Mrs. Hjodis Tersmeden of Sweden. Two girls were added to the family, and the couple remained married until his death in 1983.

★

Laurence Olivier

L aurence Olivier has been called the greatest classical player and
Shakespearean actor of the past century. Hailed as a brilliant
performer by both British and American stage and film critics,
Olivier was a skilled craftsman and dedicated professional who was
unmatched in his ability to make any role he played a memorable
event. He debuted on stage at the age of nine and appeared in his last
film, *War Requiem,* in 1989, the year of his death. During his career,
which spanned more than six decades, he directed 38 plays, 6 films,
and 6 television shows, performed 121 stage roles, and appeared in 58
films, 15 television programs, and 42 radio programs.

Laurence Kerr Olivier was born in Dorking, Surrey, England, on 22
May 1907. He was the son of the Reverend Gerald Kerr Olivier, an
Anglo-Catholic clergyman who hoped that Laurence would study for

(Photofest)

the ministry. It was in the ritual music and liturgy of the church that Olivier discovered his love of theater.

He attended All Saints Choir School in London, where he made his stage debut. Later, in April 1922, while a student at Oxford's St. Edward's school, the fifteen-year-old Olivier acted in his first play as Katharine in an all-boys production of *The Taming of the Shrew* at Stratford-on-Avon. He was already an experienced and noted actor in theater and film at the start of World War II, having joined London's Old Vic Repertory in 1937. However, his Hollywood films *Wuthering Heights* and *Rebecca* (both 1939), *Pride and Prejudice* (1940), and *That Hamilton Woman* (1941) made him, within a matter of just a few years, a glamorous Hollywood star.

Olivier and his friend, actress Vivien Leigh, were guests aboard a yacht chartered by Douglas Fairbanks, Jr., and his wife over the Labor Day weekend in 1939. Also on board were David Niven and Nigel Bruce, and while breakfasting off Catalina Island they listened to the radio as Neville Chamberlain declared war on Germany.

Niven left almost immediately, but Olivier was in the midst of filming *Rebecca* for Alfred Hitchcock and wanted to wait until his divorce from his first wife, Jill Esmond, was final so that he could marry Vivien Leigh before returning to England. Olivier had met Leigh on the set of *Fire over England* in 1937. Although he had been encouraged to remain in America and make goodwill films, Olivier wanted a more active part in the war. He married Leigh on 21 August 1940, and they sailed for neutral Lisbon aboard the American liner *Excambion* on 27 December. The hazardous transatlantic journey went without incident, but they flew into Bristol from Lisbon during an air raid, arriving in London in January 1941. Olivier, trained as a pilot in the United States, promptly applied to the Royal Air Force but was rejected because of a minor ear injury. He then applied to the Admiralty for a commission.

Initially rejected for the Fleet Air Arm because of a nerve defect in his inner ear, Olivier persisted, and thanks to the support of fellow actor Ralph Richardson, who was already in the Royal Navy, he was accepted into the Fleet Air Arm. In mid-April 1941 he was commissioned a sub-lieutenant in the Royal Navy Volunteer Reserve. After three weeks' training, learning to fly military planes at HMS *Daedalus,* a Royal Navy Air Station located near Lee-on-the-Solent, he was posted in May 1941 to Squadron 757 (HMS *Kestrel*), at Worthy Down

Olivier in an early movie, *Clouds over Europe* (1939), about stealing British aircraft secrets. Little did he know that he would be back in an aircraft cockpit during World War II. In 1941, Olivier was commissioned as a sub-lieutenant in the Fleet Air Arm and assigned to Squadron 757 at HMS *Kestral,* a training school for aerial gunners. (Photofest)

near Winchester, which was a training school for aerial gunners. Olivier was tasked with taking students up in outdated biplanes, Blackburn Sharks, while the fledgling gunners fired at ground targets and sleeves towed behind other aircraft.

Olivier experienced a rather disastrous beginning at his new post. On his first flight he prepared for takeoff without waiting for the front wheel chocks to be pulled away. As he revved up the engine to take off, the plane jumped the chocks and spun around, crashing into an adjacent plane. After this incident Olivier was tagged as a less than competent pilot. It didn't help matters much when he destroyed five more planes during the next seven weeks. Finally, in the summer of 1941, his commanding officer grounded him, and he was temporarily assigned to repacking parachutes used by the trainees during their jump exercises. Having enjoyed many stage and screen successes before joining the Royal Navy, Olivier was frustrated with this situation and began to believe that he could make a greater contribution to the war effort as an actor than as a second-line pilot.

Olivier had already appeared at rallies, given recruitment speeches, and narrated propaganda films when the Ministry of Information arranged for him to take an extended leave from the Navy in order to perform in two films in 1943. *The Demi-Paradise* (U.S. title, *Adventure for Two*) was intended to foster Anglo-Soviet relations, and *Henry V* was designed to bolster the morale of the English people. It was also the first successful Shakespeare film that Olivier produced, directed, and had a leading role in.

With the completion of *Henry V* in mid-1944, Olivier decided to leave the Navy. He resigned on 12 May 1944, with the rank of temporary lieutenant (A) (for Air Branch). Ralph Richardson resigned the same day. Olivier assisted in reviving the Old Vic Theatre Company in August 1944. He spent the remainder of the war performing and entertaining troops in England and later, after the war, in France.

Olivier was knighted in 1947, and in 1948 he won an Oscar for Best Actor for *Hamlet*. He starred in *Richard III* in 1955 and was director of the National Theatre Company in London from 1962 to 1973. His later films included *Sleuth* (1973), *Marathon Man* (1976), *A Bridge Too Far* (1977), and *The Boys from Brazil* (1978).

Laurence Olivier's awards are numerous: a Special Academy Award, and Best Actor, New York Film Critics, for *Henry V* (1946); Best Actor Academy Award, and Best Actor, New York Film Critics, for *Hamlet* (1948); Best British Actor, British Academy of Film and Television Arts (BAFTA), for *Richard III* (1955); Best Supporting Actor, New York Film Critics, for *Oh! What a Lovely War* (1969); Best Actor, New York Film Critics, for *Sleuth* (1972); and a Special Academy Award "for the full body of his work, for the unique achievements of his entire career and his lifetime contribution to the art of film" (1978).

Olivier was made Baron Olivier of Brighton (the first actor to be given this honor) in 1970. He received honorary doctorates from the universities of Oxford in 1957, Edinburgh in 1964, London in 1968, Manchester in 1969, and Sussex in 1978. He published his autobiography, *Confessions of an Actor,* in 1982.

Laurence Olivier died in Dorking, Surrey, on 11 July 1989 and is buried in Westminster Abbey.

★

Peter O'Toole

Immmortalized for his role as T. E. Lawrence in David Lean's masterpiece, *Lawrence of Arabia* (1962), Peter O'Toole has gained international fame, if not an Academy Award, despite seven Oscar nominations.

Born on 2 August 1932 in the Connemara region of Ireland, Peter Seamus O'Toole was the son of a migratory bookmaker known around the racetracks as "Captain Paddy." The family moved from County Kerry to Dublin, then to Gainsborough in Lincolnshire, England, and finally settled in Leeds in northern England. O'Toole remembers his early years as "happy," and though often lacking food at the family table and sometimes suffering a scarcity of beds, the immigrants of the Irish neighborhood took care of each other. It seemed that much time was spent at wakes or weddings, an Irish tradition that contin-

(Photofest)

O'Toole in a scene from *Lawrence of Arabia* (1962). For his performance he was nominated for a Best Actor Oscar. O'Toole served in
the Royal Navy for one year as a signalman assigned to a submarine
flotilla. (Photofest)

ues today in Irish communities in the United States. Besides spending
time with his father at the tracks, the young O'Toole would often be
smuggled into pubs under his father's coat. At the age of six he saw
Rudolf Friml's operetta *Rose Marie* and afterward fancied that he
might like to become an actor.

O'Toole received little formal education—two years at Saint
Anne's in Leeds before quitting—and at an early age joined the
work force wrapping cartons in a warehouse. He next tried jour-
nalism, hiring on as a copyboy and photographer's assistant at the
Yorkshire Evening News. During the four years he worked at the
newspaper he appeared in amateur theatricals. However, shortly
after leaving the *Evening News* he was drafted into compulsory conscripted National Service in 1952. He joined the Royal Navy and
served a one-year tour in a submarine flotilla. He wore crossed flags
with no legend above his uniform badge, which meant that he was
a signalman, a seaman who could send and receive semaphore code.

However, while at sea he was never called upon to display his skill in his rating.

While with the flotilla he went to sea on the flotilla's depot ship. He remembers these cruises in the North Atlantic with great fondness, writing in his autobiography, "There had been times of stillness, times of friendship, times of thoughtfulness, vigorous times, uncertain times, hilarious times, and times of wonder and great beauty."

O'Toole served aboard various shore stations before departing the service when his two-year tour ended. In addition to his normal naval duties ashore, he marched as a bass drummer and played rugby. Deciding to become a serious career actor, he took a scholarship to the Royal Academy of Dramatic Arts, where his classmates included Albert Finney, Alan Bates, and Richard Harris.

Following experience with the Bristol Old Vic and the Royal Shakespeare Company, O'Toole made his film debut in *The Savage Innocents* (1959). Besides *Lawrence of Arabia,* he earned Oscar nominations for *Becket* (1964), *The Lion in Winter* (1968), *Goodbye Mister Chips* (1969), *The Ruling Class* (1972), *The Stunt Man* (1980), and *My Favorite Year* (1982).

Donald Pleasence

Best remembered for his role as the obsessed Dr. Loomis in five *Halloween* movies, Donald Pleasence was born on 5 October 1919 in Worksop, Nottinghamshire, on the border of the legendary Sherwood Forest of Robin Hood fame. He came from a railway family: his grandfather was a signalman, and his father and older brother were stationmasters. He grew up in a succession of railway stations, left school at the age of seventeen, and worked for the railroad, eventually becoming manager of a station at Swinton, Yorkshire. However, he wanted to be an actor, so much so that his parents paid for elocution lessons for him.

His first stage performance was as Caesar in a student production of *Caesar and Cleopatra*. He found work in small local productions, and his persistence paid off when he was hired as assistant stage man-

(Photofest)

Pleasence as a prisoner of war at Luft Stalag 1 in northern Germany. In early 1941 he enlisted in the RAF and was trained as a radio operator in a bomber squadron. When his Lancaster bomber was shot down over France, he was captured and sent to Luft Stalag 1, where he spent a year before being repatriated. (Angela Pleasence)

ager of a theater on the channel island of Jersey. He made his stage debut in 1942 in *Wuthering Heights* and his London debut in *Twelfth Night* in 1946, and went on to gain fame as a character actor on the stage, in movies, and on television during a fifty-year career.

Pleasence registered as a conscientious objector at the beginning of the war and was sent to work as a lumberjack in the Lake District. Early in 1941 he changed his mind and enlisted in the Royal Air Force. After training, he was assigned as a radio operator in a bomber squadron. During a mission over France, Pleasence's Lancaster bomber was shot down, and he was captured and sent to a POW camp, Luft

Stalag 1, in northern Germany, where he spent a year before being repatriated. It was a role he would play realistically years later in the film *The Great Escape* (1963). Upon the camp's liberation, Pleasence was sent to a rehabilitation camp in Wolverhampton for six months before being discharged as a flight lieutenant in June 1946.

After the war, Pleasence returned to the London theater. He visited the United States for the first time in 1951 while touring with Laurence Olivier and Vivien Leigh in the stage production of *Caesar and Cleopatra*. He returned to London following the tour in America and continued to give highly acclaimed performances on the London stage.

In 1954 he made his film debut in the British production of *The Beachcomber,* which starred Charles Laughton and Elsa Lanchester. Over the next forty years he appeared in 170 films, both British and American, and performed in numerous television shows such as *The Twilight Zone* and *The Outer Limits.* His most notable films include *The Great Escape* (1963), *The Eagle Has Landed* (1976), and *The House of Usher* (1990).

Pleasence was a superb actor. His distinctive bald pate, sometimes unexpected mannerisms, and eyes that seemed to glint in a world all his own made him an arresting character. In his early career he was often cast as something of a weakling, but as his acting matured he became a master of villainous roles.

Donald Pleasence died at the age of seventy while recovering from heart valve surgery on 2 February 1995, in Saint-Paul-de-Vince in the south of France. He was survived by his fourth wife and five daughters. He died before the release of the last of the *Halloween* series, *Halloween 6* (1996).

Anthony Quayle

John Anthony Quayle was born in September 1913 in Ainsdale, Lancashire, England, to Arthur and Ester Quayle. Although Arthur was a lawyer and many family members and relatives were either doctors or lawyers, young Quayle showed no interest in these professions. His heart was set on acting and writing. Luckily, his father was an avid fan of the theater.

Following the completion of his studies at the Ruby School in 1930, Quayle briefly attended the Royal Academy of Dramatic Arts, then struck out on his own, finding small parts in various productions. He joined the famed Old Vic Company in September 1932 and periodically performed in revivals in the West End theater district of London. In 1936 he debuted on the American stage in the Broadway production of *The Country Wife*. He returned to England and the Old Vic

(Photofest)

Company and for most of 1939 toured the continent performing in Shakespearean productions.

When Britain declared war on Germany in September 1939, Quayle was a veteran actor who had spent the better part of ten years on the stage. Returning from a Mediterranean tour with the Old Vic Company as the war began, he immediately enlisted in the Royal Artillery and was posted to an officer training unit at Plymouth and then to Shoeburyness, where he received his commission as a second lieutenant. His initial posting was to a territorial unit, the Hampshire Heavy Regiment, which was tasked with manning forts as a part of Britain's coastal defenses. As German forces advanced through the Low Countries and France, Britain began to fortify itself for a possible German invasion. Quayle found the duty boring, and having endured months of wet and cold nonactivity during 1940, he vowed to seek a more exciting posting. A call came for volunteers for Hong Kong, duty that greatly appealed to him, and he signed up for the posting. Being stationed at a fort surrounded by water, he had to depend on a duty boat to get him ashore in time to join the volunteer group. The boat was behind schedule, and when he arrived at Woolwich, his would-be mates had departed for Hong Kong. However, in the spring of 1940 he volunteered for duty on Gibraltar and was soon on his way to "the Rock."

Quayle was put in charge of two 6-pound guns that overlooked the harbor. He soon found that his new duties were much like those he had left behind in England. When France surrendered, Gibraltar was overwhelmed with evacuees. During this rather frantic time, Quayle was able to spend an evening with Somerset Maugham on a coal boat.

A new second in command, Gen. Mason Macfarlane, arrived in Gibraltar, and Quayle got to know him quite well during the general's frequent inspections of the fortress defenses. Macfarlane learned that the young lieutenant was Quayle the actor and arranged for him to become aide-de-camp to the governor when the position became open. The governor, Gen. Sir Clive Liddell, was subsequently ordered back to England, and Quayle went with him. He next volunteered for Special Forces, an elite secret unit that was to organize a resistance movement should Britain be invaded. After a year with Special Forces he returned to Gibraltar as military assistant to General Macfarlane, who

Quayle dancing with his wife, actress Dorothy Hyson, at a party following the premiere of *Lawrence of Arabia*. When war broke out
with Germany, Quayle enlisted in the Royal Artillery and after officer
training at Plymouth and Shoeburyness, he was commissioned a second lieutenant. He was initially posted to the Hampshire Heavy Regiment, a territorial unit that manned forts as part of Britain's coastal
defense. Quayle later assumed similar duty in Gibraltar and eventually
served in Britain's elite Special Forces. (Photofest)

was assigned as the new governor of the outpost. Quayle was excited
by this new duty, since Gibraltar had become a key supply and planning base for Operation Torch, the forthcoming invasion of North
Africa. Because of his position Quayle was able to meet many of the
dominant Allied leaders, including General Eisenhower, Prime Minister Churchill, and generals Marshall and De Gaulle.

Later in 1943 the Special Operations Executive needed men in the
Balkans to set up bases that could be used to distribute arms and
equipment to partisans who were fighting Germans occupying Albanian territory. Quayle volunteered, and after parachute and demolitions

training he entered Albania by a small fishing boat, the *Sea Maid,* from Brindisi, Italy. He was ordered to take charge of an area south of the port of Valona, where a small Allied base called Sea View had been established. Quayle's orders were to conduct reconnaissance, kill Germans, and help the partisans.

Upon arriving at the base, Quayle ran into a rather complicated situation. Communist partisans were battling the Germans with Allied-provided weapons, but they were also fighting their political opponents, the right-wing Balli Kombetar. Quayle soon learned that the country was on the verge of a civil war. Although the Balli forces provided intelligence and kept the whereabouts of Quayle's base and his men a secret, they would not fight the Germans, since they knew that once the Allies had won the war, they would need all their resources to fight the communist partisans. One of the first things Quayle did was to establish another base just in case Sea View was compromised. He chose a site to the south of Grama. It proved to be a wise decision, since shortly thereafter Sea View was deluged with Italians trying to escape the Germans following Italy's surrender. Some forty thousand Italian soldiers had already been deported to Germany.

Early on, Quayle made contact with the communist commissar of the 5th Partisan Brigade in hopes that he might get the two sides together to focus on the common enemy. As the negotiations began, the commissar requested more arms and asked that they not pass through Sea View, since that was in Balli territory. He suggested a beach site south of Vuno that was controlled by his own forces. Quayle went to the site and approved it. He returned to the 5th Brigade base and voiced his decision, then went on to Grama to arrange for the transport of the weapons from Italy to the beach area. Shortly after reaching Grama he was informed that German troops were approaching the base and that his unit must move immediately. Quayle and his men grabbed what they could and scrambled up the mountain adjacent to the base. Climbing was slow, since they had to dig their fingers into the ground, and the shale kept giving way beneath their boots. Someone yelled that figures could be seen in the camp, and Quayle was certain that he and his men would be killed by enemy fire. However, there were no shots coming from the camp below, and they made it to a high ridge, where they hid for the night. Looking down on the camp, they saw that it was deserted, and they cautiously descended. The camp was completely ransacked. The warning had been a ruse.

The location of Grama was now known to the fleeing Italians, and many entered the camp hoping to be transported across the Adriatic Sea to their homeland. It was January 1944; heavy rain and snow fell day after day, making life miserable for Quayle and his men. The fighting continued between the partisan adversaries, and Quayle gave up all hope of organizing a concerted effort. Then, reliable information was received that German forces were advancing on the camp. Quayle and his group again scampered up the mountain, where they found a cave that provided shelter and a safe hiding place. For the next few weeks he and his men moved through the mountains meeting and talking with partisan groups in an effort to cajole them into joining together in fighting the German forces that were now retreating north from Greece. Their efforts were to no avail. Frustrated and depressed with their failure to carry out their mission, they continued on until Quayle contracted malaria and was evacuated back to Italy. After a month in a hospital, Quayle was well enough to return to the Albanian mountains to gather his men and bring them back to safety. There was little to show for their three-month operation. They never were able to solve the partisan problem and did little in the way of sabotage. However, they did keep a German brigade occupied with trying to track them down.

Quayle was discharged in 1945 and returned to the theater. Among his many movies, one, *The Guns of Navarone* (1961), brought back memories of his Balkan experience. The story line in the movie included a landing by a fishing boat, the scaling of cliffs, and the hardships endured by a small group of Allied soldiers as they attacked a German target in the Balkans.

After the war Quayle managed the Shakespeare Memorial Theatre Company of Stratford-on-Avon from 1948 to 1956. While there he attracted to Stratford renowned actors such as Laurence Olivier, John Gielgud, Ralph Richardson, and Margaret Leighton. During the ensuing years he made many stage appearances in New York and London. He realized his only box-office smash hit when he appeared in *Sleuth* (1970), which first opened in London's West End and then went on to Broadway. During his career he performed in thirty movies, including *Lawrence of Arabia* (1962); *Anne of the Thousand Days* (1969), for which he was nominated for an Academy Award for Best Supporting Actor; and *The Eagle Has Landed* (1976), which starred Michael Caine, Donald Sutherland, and Robert Duvall. Quayle was knighted in 1985. He directed his own touring company until July 1989 and died in London in October of that year.

Sir Anthony Quayle has been called one of the English-speaking world's most distinguished classical actors.

Chips Rafferty

T he Australian actor who came to symbolize the stereotypical "Aussie," Chips Rafferty was born John William Pilbean Goffage in Broken Hill, New South Wales, on 26 March 1909. Broken Hill was at the time primarily a mining community located in the center of the Outback. He graduated from Parramatta High School in 1927. Like most actors of the day, Rafferty got his start on the stage, appearing in numerous productions before being cast in his first film, *Ants in His Pants* (1940), followed by *Forty Thousand Horsemen* (1941).

During World War II, Rafferty served as a flight lieutenant in the Royal Australian Air Force and was stationed on Morotai in the southwestern Pacific, one of the largest air bases in the area. Squadrons from Morotai and neighboring Noemfoor were charged with pro-

(Photofest)

Rafferty in *The Desert Rats* (1963). At the outbreak of World War II, he enlisted in the Royal Australian Air Force, where he was commissioned as a pilot officer. Rafferty served more than four years in Australia and New Guinea. (Photofest)

tecting Gen. Douglas MacArthur's western flank during the Allied advance on the Philippines. When Australian actor Bill Cosgrove crashed his Beaufighter into the sea in 1943, it was Rafferty who discovered the wreckage.

Rafferty was allowed to perform in films during his military service, appearing in the morale-building *The Rats of Tobruk* in 1944 and *The Overlanders* in 1945. He returned to acting following the war, often playing soldiers. In 1953 he appeared in *The Desert Rats,* with Richard Burton and James Mason, portraying a member of the 9th Australian Division at Tobruk during the 242-day siege by Rommel's Afrika Korps.

Rafferty's other notable films include *Eureka Stockade* (1949), with Peter Finch; *The Wackiest Ship in the Army* (1960), with Jack Lemmon; *The Sundowners* (1960), with Deborah Kerr; *Mutiny on the*

Bounty (1962), with Marlon Brando; and *Double Trouble* (1967), with Elvis Presley. His last film, *Outback* (1971), also known as *Wake in Fright*, was completed shortly before his death from a heart attack on a Sydney street on 27 May 1971.

During his long and successful screen career, he was recognized at home and abroad as Australia's best-known film actor. In 1989, Rafferty and three others—Charles Chauvel, Lottie Lyell, and Raymond Longford—were depicted on an Australian postage stamp honoring early Australian cinema.

Claude Rains

T he image produced at the mention of the name Claude Rains might be indistinct in the minds of many, but utter the phrase "Round up the usual suspects," and the haziness resolves into a clear picture of Capt. Louis Renault, the Vichy police chief in *Casablanca* (1943), with Humphrey Bogart, perhaps Rains's best-known role. In a film career that spanned over thirty years and included four Oscar nominations for Best Supporting Actor, Rains consistently worked with some of the finest talents in some of the best films of his time.

He was born William Claude Rains in London on 10 November 1889, son of Frederick William and Emily Eliza (Cox) Rains. His father was a popular stage actor and pioneer filmmaker who acted in, directed, and produced over five hundred early motion pictures. Thus, when young Claude enjoyed his first stage success at age ten with a

(Photofest)

part in the choir for a performance of *Sweet Nell of Old Drury* at London's Haymarket Theatre on 31 August 1900, it was not difficult to get his parents' permission to leave school for a job at His Majesty's Theatre. During his seven years there, he worked in nearly every job, from call boy to prompter, stage manager to company manager, earning a comprehensive education in the technical side of his craft.

On 28 June 1911, at age twenty-one, Rains had his adult stage debut in Dunsany's *Gods of the Mountain*. Later that year he toured Australia with a production of *The Blue Bird*. By 1913 he was on tour in America as stage manager of the Granville-Barker Repertory Company. While on this tour, Rains made his American stage debut, but with news of war in Europe, he began plans to return to England, arriving in early 1915.

Rains enlisted in the 1/14th Battalion London (Scotts) Regiment because he saw a Scottish soldier attired in a "gorgeous tartan" kilt and was impressed with how smart the uniform looked. He would find, however, that the uniform came with a price. The London Scottish was the 1st Territorial Infantry Battalion in action against the Germans at Messines on 31 October 1914, and it served in Flanders and France throughout the war.

Most likely, the first part of Rains's service was spent in the static trench warfare of the Western Front. In March 1916 the British forces took over responsibility for the Arras sector from the French. The Germans had occupied the Vimy Ridge, about seven miles northeast of Arras, since September 1914. The French had tried twice, unsuccessfully, to dislodge the Germans from the strategically located heights. Now it was Britain's turn.

On 9 April 1917, British forces attacked in the Arras sector, and Rains was gassed (some accounts say wounded) at Vimy Ridge and evacuated back to England. Rains would later credit the gassing for the unique timbre in his voice as well as for his being nearly blind in one eye. The Canadians would capture the ridge, but at great cost.

After recovering, Rains was posted to the Bedford Regiment, where he finished the war, being discharged in 1919 with the rank of captain. Although he considered making the Army a career, he found the call of the theater too enticing, and he returned to the stage. While continuing to play the title role in *Julius Caesar* and Napoleon in *Man of Destiny*, he took a position as an instructor at the Royal Academy of Dramatic

Rains as Capt. Louis Renault, the Vischy police chief in *Casablanca* (1942), telling one of his men to "round up the usual suspects." In 1914 Rains enlisted in the 1/14th Battalion London (Scottish) Regiment, the first territorial infantry battalion in action against the Germans at Messines. During the war he served in Flanders and in France, and was gassed and wounded in action. (Photofest)

Arts in 1922, where he tutored a student with promise, Laurence Olivier. He also married one of his students, Beatriz Thomas, in 1926, but the marriage ended in divorce when, while on tour together in an American production of *The Constant Nymph,* he decided to remain in the United States and she decided to return home to England.

Rains had already played several roles on Broadway when he was given a three-year contract (later extended to five) with the New York Theater Guild. In 1933 a screen test with Universal led to his being offered the lead in the film *The Invisible Man.* Since the character he portrayed was "invisible," it was clearly Rains's distinctive voice that got him the part. It would be the first in a long line of distinguished performances on film. Although *The Invisible Man* is considered his film debut, he actually appeared in his first film, *Build Thy House,* in 1920.

Many forgettable films followed, and some unforgettable, like *Four*

Daughters (1938) and its sequel, *Daughters Courageous* (1939), as well as *The Adventures of Robin Hood* (1938), in which he played the villainous Prince John. He played Napoleon III in *Juarez* (1939), and 1939 was the year he received his first Best Supporting Actor nomination, for his portrayal of Senator Joseph Payne in Frank Capra's *Mr. Smith Goes to Washington,* with Jimmy Stewart.

Subsequent Best Supporting Actor nominations included his portrayal of Capt. Louis Renault in *Casablanca* (1943), which won the Best Picture Oscar; *Mr. Skeffington* (1944), one of four films in which he would co-star with Bette Davis; and Alfred Hitchcock's *Notorious* (1946), a spy thriller with Cary Grant and Ingrid Bergman.

Other notable roles include the lead in *Here Comes Mr. Jordan* (1941); *Kings Row* (1942); *Phantom of the Opera* (1943); *Caesar and Cleopatra* (1946), in which he played Julius Caesar (and became the first actor ever paid $1 million for a role); and *Robin Hood* (1947), in which he reprised his role as Prince John.

He returned to Broadway in 1951 with the highly successful and well-received *Darkness at Noon,* but he continued to make films throughout the 1950s and 1960s, most notably playing the mayor in *The Pied Piper of Hamlin* (1957); Mr. Dryden in *Lawrence of Arabia* (1962), with Peter O'Toole and Omar Sharif, which won an Oscar for Best Picture; and King Herod in *The Greatest Story Ever Told* (1965), his final film.

Rains also made numerous appearances on the relatively new medium of television, appearing as a guest on shows like *Rawhide, Wagon Train,* and *Dr. Kildare* and making several appearances for his friend on *Alfred Hitchcock Presents.*

In his personal life, suffice it to say that he had a fondness for the ladies. He was married six times in his seventy-seven years, mostly to younger women. This fact once prompted four-time co-star Bette Davis to quip, when asked if Rains had ever made romantic moves on her, "Oh heavens, no! I was nineteen years younger than Claude. Much too old for him."

Claude Rains died of "internal bleeding" on 30 May 1967 in Laconia, New Hampshire. During his career he never stopped working, playing both starring and supporting roles as villains, monsters, heroes, lovers, and kings.

Basil Rathbone

"Elementary my dear Watson, elementary." These characteristic words were often spoken to his sidekick by Basil Rathbone, the most memorable Sherlock Holmes of the 1930s and 1940s. Performing the role both on radio and in sixteen films, he played a convincing, cunning, and aloof detective of unmatched skill, a source of continuing surprise to a bumbling Dr. Watson. His superb performances in such tales as *The Hound of the Baskervilles* (1939), *The Adventures of Sherlock Holmes* (1939), which also starred actress Ida Lupino, and *The House of Fear* (1945) continue to be shown on cable channels today and reflect the unique skills of the movie makers of that era.

Critics have often remarked that Rathbone was an actor who appeared to have been born and trained for the role of Sir Arthur Conan Doyle's Sherlock Holmes. But Rathbone was more than a series

(Photofest)

actor. He appeared in more than eighty films during his forty-year theatrical career and was nominated for Academy Awards for Best Supporting Actor for *Romeo and Juliet* in 1936 and *If I Were King* in 1938. He became the ideal film enemy of such leading Hollywood swashbucklers as Errol Flynn and Tyrone Power.

Basil Rathbone was born on 13 June 1892 to Edgar Philip and Anna Barbara (George) Rathbone in Johannesburg, South Africa, the oldest of three children. His father was a mining engineer, employed in South Africa at the time. The family was forced to flee the country after his father was accused of being a British spy by the Boers in 1895. Rathbone was brought up in England, where in time he was enrolled at Repton School, receiving a classical education in Latin and Greek. A mediocre student, he excelled in music and sports. He was unaware that his ancestry included authors on his paternal side (English and Scottish) and poets, dramatists, and actors on his maternal side (Irish). Upon his graduation in 1910 at the age of eighteen, his father obtained a position for him with the Globe Insurance Company in Liverpool, but he left the company after a year to join the theatrical company of his cousin, Sir Fred Benson.

Rathbone's first stage appearance was as Hortensio in a Theatre Royal performance of Shakespeare's *The Taming of the Shrew* in April 1911. The following year he toured America with Benson's Number 2 Shakespearean Company, performing forty-seven roles in twenty-two Shakespearean plays. After returning to England he continued to tour with Benson's company.

With the start of World War I, Rathbone was anxious to do his part, and he enlisted in the British Army in June 1915. Private Rathbone completed his basic infantry training in London, then applied and was accepted for officer training. Sent to Scotland, he completed his training and was commissioned a second lieutenant and at his request was assigned to the 2nd Battalion, Liverpool, Scottish Regiment.

The regiment was assigned as part of the 57th Division and was held in England for several months before being sent overseas to France. In September 1918 Rathbone was awarded the Military Cross for his actions during a reconnaissance mission while serving as an intelligence officer. In his words, "All I did was disguise myself as a tree and cross no man's land to gather a bit of information from the

Rathbone was the most memorable Sherlock Holmes of the thirties and forties, and his Holmes films, many considered classics, are still shown on cable channels. He served in World War I as a second lieutenant in the 2nd Battalion, Liverpool, Scottish Regiment. He saw combat in France and was awarded the Military Cross for his actions during a reconnaissance mission. (Photofest)

German lines. I have not since been called upon to play a tree."

While Rathbone came through the war relatively unscathed, his mother died in 1917 while he was overseas, and his brother John was killed while serving with the Dorset Regiment on 4 June 1918. It was his war service and the death of his brother that contributed to his decision to remain a British citizen after moving to the United States.

After the war Rathbone resumed his career in the theater, performing Shakespeare at Stratford-on-Avon. He traveled to New York City in 1924 and played romantic leads on Broadway throughout the 1920s. He moved to Hollywood in 1935 and became noted in the early Hollywood community for his lavish parties attended by the most notable screen celebrities.

Rathbone's first film appearance was in the MGM production of *The Masked Bride* (1925). During the years leading up to his performance in the Sherlock Holmes series, he divided his time between Hollywood, the New York stage, and engagements in England performing in plays such as *The Barretts of Wimpole Street,* opposite famed actress Katherine Cornell, and *Romeo and Juliet.* His cinema appearances continued well beyond his Sherlock Holmes series. His most notable films include *A Tale of Two Cities* (1935), with Ronald Colman; *The Adventures of Robin Hood* (1938), with Errol Flynn; *Dawn Patrol* (1938), again with Errol Flynn; *The Mark of Zorro* (1940), with Tyrone Power; *Above Suspicion* (1943), with Joan Crawford; *Frenchman's Creek* (1944), with Joan Fontaine; *We're No Angels* (1955), with Humphrey Bogart; *The Court Jester* (1956), with Danny Kaye; and *The Last Hurrah* (1958), with Spencer Tracy.

Rathbone attempted to enlist following the start of World War II in September 1939, but he was turned down by the War Office in London as being too old, so he spent the war years entertaining troops at the Hollywood Canteen and serving as president of British War Relief in Los Angeles.

During the 1960s Rathbone continued to act on the stage and in films and to give readings around the country. His reading of the Oscar Wilde poem "The Nightingale and the Rose" was judged by the *New York World-Telegram and Sun* as "one of the most gripping solo performances read this season in Carnegie Hall."

In his later years Rathbone lived in a brownstone in New York City with his wife Quide Begere, whom he had married in the late 1920s, and his daughter Cynthia. His wife was the author of several plays and screen adaptations and was a story editor for Paramount Studios. He had a son from a former marriage who served in the Royal Air Force in the 1950s.

Rathbone published an autobiography, *In and out of Character,* in 1962 and died in New York City on 21 July 1967.

★

Michael Rennie

W hen director Robert Wise selected Michael Rennie, over
Claude Rains, for the role of Klaatu, the alien emissary in
the film *The Day the Earth Stood Still* (1951), it was surely
because he felt that Rennie could better project the mystery and oth-
erworldliness of the character. Mystery was always an essential ele-
ment of the Rennie persona. He was an intensely private man, and certain mysteries surround him more than thirty years after his death.
Why was an actor who loved, and was loved by, so many women
offered so few romantic leads? Why was so versatile and talented an
actor so underrated and unappreciated in his time? And what did he
really do during World War II?

Michael Rennie was born Eric Alexander Rennie in Bradford, West
Yorkshire, England, on 25 August 1909 (some accounts say 1910, but

(Photofest)

military records and a graveside memorial give 1909 as the year of his birth). His early life was middle class, and he was educated at the Oatlands Preparatory School in Harrogate before matriculating at the Leys School, Cambridge, which he attended from April 1924 to December 1926. Despite what later studio publicity releases would suggest, the Leys School had nothing to do with Cambridge University.

The expectation was that Rennie would go to work in the family's 150-year-old wool business, W. M. Rennie and Company, and he did for a time but left to pursue his dream of a career on stage. He acted in the Yorkshire Stock Company and the York Repertory Company, performing contemporary works, while supporting himself as a car salesman and sometime factory manager.

In the early 1930s Rennie began acting in British films, as a bit player and extra and as a stand-in. He recalled preferring work as a stand-in, as it allowed him to remain on the set, observing how movies were put together, for as long as the filming continued, as opposed to the one or two days that would have been required of him in a bit part. Nonetheless, by the mid-1930s Rennie was appearing regularly in small parts. His early films included *Murder in Diamond Row* (1937), *Bank Holiday* (1938), *The Divorce of Lady X* (1938), and *This Man in Paris* (1939), among others. His first featured role was in *Ships with Wings* (1941), and his first lead came that same year when he played a British spy in *Tower of Terror.*

With the start of World War II, the mystery of Rennie's military service also began. He stated that everyone dangled contracts before him after *Ships with Wings,* but he enlisted in the Royal Air Force on 3 September 1939. What makes this interesting is that *Ships with Wings* was not released until 1941, and the studio had him enlisting on the very day war was declared in Europe.

According to available RAF records, Eric Alexander Rennie enlisted in the Royal Air Force Volunteer Reserve on 27 May 1941, becoming RAFVR #1391153. He was discharged for commission on 4 August 1942 and the next day was commissioned "for the emergency" as a pilot officer (#127347) on probation in the General Duties Branch of the RAFVR. On 5 February 1943 he was promoted to flying officer on probation, and he resigned his commission on 1 May 1944.

It is also known that Rennie took basic training at Torquay,

Not much is known about Rennie's wartime experiences because his records are not available. He enlisted in the Royal Air Force Volunteer Reserve in 1941 and was commissioned a year later. On 5 February 1943, he was promoted to flying officer. Reliable sources confirm that he took flight training in Macon, Georgia, after which he returned to England and joined a bomber squadron. He resigned his commission on 1 May 1944. (Michael Rennie collection)

Devon, and that he was temporarily released from duty to appear in the all-star propaganda film *The Big Blockade* (1942). He took flight training in England, Canada, and the United States (Georgia), was classified as being too old to fly, and spent the next two and a half years as a flight instructor in Macon, Georgia, assigned with the U.S. Army Air Corps. He contracted a skin ailment in Florida and was released from service.

The RAF stated, "[We] can confirm that Flying Officer Rennie was not invalided out of the Royal Air Force, and that he did not see active service or qualify as a pilot instructor." It is clear that although numerous newspaper and magazine articles suggest that he was discharged on medical grounds (the skin ailment), this was not the case, nor was he an instructor pilot in Georgia or anywhere else. It is not surprising that Hollywood publicists might exaggerate their clients' war service, but what are the facts?

It is likely that Rennie did come to Georgia for flight training as a pilot candidate, for at this time Britain was training potential pilots overseas (primarily in South Africa, Canada, and the United States) because of the lack of sufficient facilities, the poor weather, and the threat of attack from enemy aircraft at home. Several individuals recall training with Rennie in Class 42-G at Macon, Georgia, in May–June 1942. Class 42-G would have graduated in July–August, about the time Rennie was commissioned a pilot officer (second lieutenant).

Ron Pickler, an RAF pilot candidate in the class behind Rennie's at Macon, recalled that Rennie was a cadet lieutenant, very popular and well liked. On one occasion the base cinema was showing *Ships with Wings,* in which Rennie had played the commander of a flight of Swordfish bombers, and Pickler recalls him taking the ribbing good-naturedly.

Earlier at Turner Field, during primary flight training, Rennie flew the Boeing PT-17 Stearman biplane. At Cochran Field, Macon, during his basic flight school, Rennie trained in the Vultee B-13A Valiant, a monoplane with a single 450-horsepower engine. He also became familiar with night, formation, and instrument flying. At the completion of his basic school, the determination would be made for further training in fighters or bombers. Pickler believes he advanced to bombers, but everything beyond this point is pure conjecture, and RAF records will not become available until after seventy-five years.

Whatever the reason, by 1945 Rennie was back in England making films, and following the end of the war he played in his first major postwar film, *Caesar and Cleopatra* (1946). The film, starring Claude Rains and Vivien Leigh, was Rennie's first experience with the Hollywood epic. This was followed by *Root of All Evil* (1947) and *The Golden Madonna* (1949). In 1950, Rennie had the role of King Edward in the 20th Century Fox historical epic *The Black Rose,* starring Tyrone Power as a medieval Saxon. His performance eventually led to a contract offer from Fox.

In 1951, Rennie had his American debut in Otto Preminger's mystery film *The Thirteenth Letter* (1951), with Charles Boyer. No one, least of all Rennie, could have foreseen that his next film would achieve classic status and grant him screen immortality. The film, *The Day the Earth Stood Still* (1951), in which Rennie played the alien ambassador Klaatu, has come to be regarded as a masterwork of the science fiction genre. Co-starring Patricia Neal, Billy Gray, and Sam Jaffe, it is considered by most to be Rennie's best work.

Other quality roles followed: the lead in the fourth incarnation of Victor Hugo's *Les Misérables* (1952) and the part of the Apostle Peter in *The Robe* (1952), with Richard Burton, Jean Simmons, and Victor Mature, a role he reprised in *Demetrius and the Gladiators* (1954). Nor was Rennie averse to taking roles in the action pictures that dominated the movie screens of the 1950s, such as *King of the Khyber Rifles* (1954), playing Tyrone Power's commanding officer; *Soldier of Fortune* (1955), with Clark Gable and Susan Hayward; and *The Devil's Brigade* (1968), playing a general.

What with poor film choices, advancing age, and the end of his Fox contract in 1958, Rennie's film career was in decline by the end of the decade. However, he took advantage of the increasing opportunities in the new medium of television. He starred in the television series *The Third Man* from 1959 to 1960 (1962 to 1965 in Britain) as private detective Harry Lime, and he made guest appearances on shows like *Lost in Space* (where he was reunited with *Third Man* co-star Jonathan Harris), *Batman, The Man from U.N.C.L.E., Wagon Train, Time Tunnel,* and several episodes of *Alfred Hitchcock Presents,* among others.

During the 1960s Rennie continued making films and television appearances, and he appeared on Broadway in the successful and critically well received comedy *Mary, Mary.* He also took up American citizenship in 1960. Afflicted by respiratory ailments, Rennie died suddenly on 19 June 1971 while visiting his aged mother in Harrogate, Yorkshire, where he was laid to rest at All Saints Church.

What lingers is the mystery of why Rennie remains so underappreciated. What best exemplifies his greatness is his versatility—the wide variety of roles in which he created such seamless characters. Whether he was playing a villainous Bedouin chieftain in *Princess of the Nile* (1954), Father Junipero Serra in *Seven Cities of Gold* (1955), or Lana Turner's playboy husband in *The Rains of Ranchipur* (1955), he had the talent to make the characters real and believable. That is perhaps the highest praise for a performer.

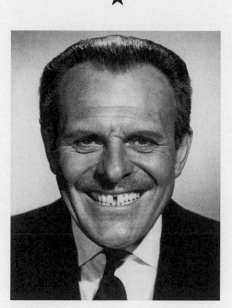

Terry-Thomas

F amous for gapped teeth beneath a guardsman mustache and for playing bumbling Englishmen of all classes, Terry-Thomas was born Thomas Terry Hoar-Stevens in Finchley, London, on 14 July 1911, the fourth of five children of a business executive. He was educated in preparatory schools and graduated from Ardingly College in Sussex in early 1928. Less than a stellar academic student, he excelled in the Officers Training Course and considered a military career but did not possess the independent income necessary for officers at the time.

He took work as a clerk and later as a salesman at the Union Cold Storage Company Smithfield Meat Market. He recalled in his autobiography that only his performances in the company's amateur productions saved him from being fired for habitual tardiness. He orga-

(Photofest)

Terry-Thomas with costars from the 1963 comedy, *It's a Mad, Mad, Mad, Mad World*. At the beginning of World War II, he enlisted as a private in the British army and was assigned to the Royal Corps of Signals. While in the army Thomas toured British bases as part of the cast of "Stars in Battledress." He was discharged on April Fool's Day, 1946, after having attained the rank of sergeant. (Photofest)

nized and played a ukelele with a band called the Rhythm Maniacs, taught dancing at the Cricklewood Palais, and did impersonations of celebrated singers. He began taking bit parts in films in 1935. He was performing in music halls and cabarets at the start of World War II in September 1939. His stage work led to his film debut as an extra in *It's Love Again* (1936). Two years later he was on radio.

Terry-Thomas enlisted in the British Army and was assigned to the Royal Corps of Signals, rising from private to sergeant before being demobilized and discharged on April Fools' Day 1946. He left the Army with four medals and a duodenal ulcer. While in the Army he toured British bases as part of the cast of "Stars in Battledress."

After leaving the Army, Terry-Thomas appeared on tour in *Piccadilly Hayride* and won recognition for his performances. He spent the next decade perfecting his craft on radio, television, stage, and film. He caught the notice of American audiences in the 1956 film *Private's Progress*, playing the part of Major Hitchcock, a blundering university student turned soldier.

Terry-Thomas appeared in over twenty-five films, including *Make Mine Mink* (1960), *It's a Mad, Mad, Mad, Mad World* (1963), *Those Magnificent Men in Their Flying Machines* (1965), and *Where Were You When the Lights Went Out?* (1968). He published an autobiography, *Filling the Gap,* in 1959. During the 1970s he worked in Italy but was forced by illness to discontinue his appearances. He died of Parkinson's disease on 8 January 1990 in Godalming, Surrey, England.

In his autobiography Terry-Thomas described himself as a bounder, aristocratic rogue, upper-class English twit, genuine English eccentric, high-bred idiot, cheeky blighter, twentieth-century dandy, amiable buffoon, and king of cads. Indeed, he played many of those roles on the screen, but underneath it all he was a gifted comedian. He captured the interest of filmgoers in America in the 1950s and 1960s with his zany antics, but the man was funny—really funny. One of his most hilarious performances was in *How to Murder Your Wife* (1965), which starred Jack Lemmon, Virna Lisi, and Eddie Mayehoff.

Richard Todd

W hen Richard Todd portrayed British glider infantry officer Maj. John Howard in the Darryl Zanuck film *The Longest Day* (1962), he brought a unique perspective to the part. One of the first paratroop officers to be dropped behind enemy lines at Normandy as part of the 7th Light Infantry Parachute Battalion prior to the invasion, Todd was with Howard the following day at the first bridge over the Orne River, helping repel a counterattack by the 12th SS Hitler Jugend Panzer Division, a scene recreated in the film.

Born Richard Andrew Palethorpe-Todd in Dublin, Ireland, on 11 June 1919, he was the son of Maj. A. W. and Marville Palethorpe-Todd. His father, an Army officer, was transferred in 1921 to India, where the family was stationed for two years before returning to Ireland. In 1925 the family moved again, this time to Devon, England.

(Photofest)

Educated by private tutors before entering a preparatory school out-side Exeter, Todd eventually graduated from Shrewsbury Public School, where he developed an interest in becoming a playwright. He had always wanted to write plays but knew nothing about the theater, so he decided to go to drama school.

He enrolled in the Italia Conti (Drama) School in London but left after six months to work in repertory and stock companies across England and Scotland getting practical theater experience. He helped found the Dundee Repertory Theatre in April 1939.

Todd was living in a little flat in Broughty Ferry when war was declared on 3 September 1939. The next day he went down to St. Andrew's University, convinced the authorities that he was a student and cadet there, and was accepted as an officer candidate. He was told to return home to await orders. As time passed and his mates were called up, Todd grew concerned and began sending letters of inquiry to the War Office. Finally, on 16 July 1940, he received his call-up and orders to report to "Volunteer—B Company" in Strensall, Yorkshire, for basic training, assigned as an officer candidate with the King's Own Yorkshire Light Infantry (KOYLI). After completing this training he attended Sandhurst for four months of precommissioning, attached to No. 16 Platoon, Company C.

While in training, he was injured when a bomb exploded in his building during an air raid. He subsequently spent time recovering in the hospital, missing his group's graduation, and was not commissioned as a second lieutenant (#180649) until the spring of 1941. He narrowly escaped death by bombardment a second time when, while in London to celebrate his "passing out" as an officer, he was unable to get into the crowded Café de Paris. He went elsewhere to celebrate, and later that evening a bomb penetrated the roof of the club he was in and exploded on the dance floor, killing eighty-four.

Todd returned to his regiment at Strensall, where he received an additional three months' training in infantry tactics and Bren-gun car-rier driving, before being assigned in the late summer of 1941 to the 2nd/4th Battalion, KOYLI, at Diddington Camp, near Swaffham, Nor-folk, where the mission was to defend the local area's airfields. From there they were posted, as part of the XII Corps under Gen. Bernard Montgomery, to Hythe, Kent, where Todd commanded the infantry

Paratrooper Richard Todd, *right,* at training camp prior to dropping behind enemy lines at Normandy as part of the 7th Light Infantry Parachute Battalion. He parachuted into France on D-Day, fought near the Orne River, and later manned the defenses on the River Meuse during the Battle of the Bulge. He was also among the Allied soldiers who met up with Russian troops on the Elbe River. After the war ended, he was assigned occupation duty in Palestine. He was discharged from the Army in August 1946. (Richard Todd collection)

contingent at Dymchurch Redoubt, a Napoleonic fortress armed with two ancient 6-inch guns. He attended one of the first "battle schools" (realistic training exercises conducted under simulated battle conditions, using live ammunition and ordnance), then attended the instructor's course, where he learned what war was about—as he put it, "stamina, exertion, fatigue, dirt, discomfort, wetness."

In December 1941, Todd was posted to the Alabaster Force at Reykjavik, Iceland, as part of the 1st/4th KOYLI, 49th Infantry Division, which supported Royal Artillery and Engineer units. The unit was trained in Arctic survival by Canadians and in mountain warfare by Norwegians.

By September of the following year, Americans had taken over for the English in Iceland, and Todd, now a lieutenant and assistant adjutant, was sent to the Battalion Signal Officers Course at the Infantry

School in Catterick, England. Although he lacked essential knowledge of the subject, his ability as an actor to memorize long passages served him well during the course, and he graduated as one of the top students, despite having never acquired the concomitant skills. Nevertheless, his scores resulted in his appointment as a signals instructor at the regimental depot at Berwick-on-Tweed.

A chance meeting with an old friend, Maj. R. B. Freeman-Thomas, rescued him from what he perceived as the "backwaters" of the war, and he was transferred in early 1943 to the headquarters staff of the 42nd Armored Division as a liaison officer. When that division was disbanded, he was assigned to the newly forming 7th Light Infantry Parachute Battalion, part of the 6th Airborne Division, which was in training for the upcoming invasion of the European mainland. In the summer of 1943 Todd reported to the parachute regiment depot at Hardwick Hall, Derbyshire. He underwent parachute training at Ringwood Airport at Manchester, then was sent to Salisbury Plain (Buford Camp) for D-Day training. As assistant adjutant, he was privy to the target information necessary for him to work on aircraft loading and equipment schedule projects. He was assigned to aircraft number 1 for the jump into Normandy, and on the evening of 5 June, as the largest armada in history sailed toward France, his unit took off into the night.

After helping secure the Caen Canal bridges (code-named Pegasus Bridge) over the Orne River, Todd commanded the battalion machine-gun and mortar unit, which, owing to the confusion of the airdrop, was without its heavy equipment and radios. On 11 June, after several days of fierce combat, Todd was relieved and sent back to division headquarters to resume his G-3 (operations) duties, and there he remained until the breakout. After his unit crossed the Seine River, he returned to England in late August 1944, but newly promoted Captain Todd was back in combat in December 1944, manning the River Meuse defenses during the Battle of the Bulge, where he operated gun jeeps, deceiving the Germans as to British strength by driving from position to position and firing his weapons. He remained with the unit as it pushed eastward, crossing the Rhine and meeting up with Russian troops on the Elbe River. Following the end of the war in Europe his unit was returned to England in mid-May 1945 via Calais.

Todd was next sent to Gaza in the Middle East for nine months, assigned to occupation duty with the 3d Parachute Brigade of the reformed 6th Airborne Division. While there he was involved in a motor vehicle accident and injured his shoulder and arm. When his unit was moved to Tel Aviv in 1946, he was shipped home and honorably demobilized from the Army that same year at Aldershot, but a large part of his future career would be spent in military uniform.

Todd returned to the Dundee Repertory Company, starring in plays like *Claudia* (where he became engaged to the leading lady, Catherine Grant-Bogle) and *The Hasty Heart,* playing the part of Yank with co-stars Ronald Reagan and Patricia Neal. In 1948 he went to London for a screen test for director Robert Lennard and was given a contract with Associated British Picture Corporation. His first picture for the company was *For Them That Trespass* (1949), in which he played a man punished for a murder he did not commit. His performance was praised by the critics.

His second film role was a reprise of his stage role in *The Hasty Heart,* this time playing Lachie, the terminally ill Scottish soldier, for which he earned a Best Actor Oscar nomination in 1950. War films were increasingly popular in both the United States and Britain during the 1950s, and many of the most popular actors—John Mills, Dirk Bogarde, Trevor Howard, and Kenneth More—brought an authenticity to their roles because of their personal experiences in the war.

Todd himself would play a variety of military roles in films. These included *The Dam Busters* (1955), about Allied efforts to destroy Germany's Ruhr Dam; *Breakout* (1959), a POW escape film with Richard Attenborough; *Jungle Fighters* (1961); *The Long, the Short, and the Tall* (1961), about British war efforts against Japan; and *Operation Crossbow* (1965), a true account of Allied efforts to destroy the German V-1 and V-2 rocket installations, with Sophia Loren, Trevor Howard, John Mills, and Anthony Quayle. In addition, there were two films about D-Day: *D-Day, the Sixth of June* (1956) and *The Longest Day* (1962). The first, a British film, was criticized for overemphasizing the British contribution, while the second, American made, was perceived, at least by Todd, as "being too much about Americans."

Other notable roles involved his playing larger-than-life characters, real and legendary, such as Robin Hood in *Robin Hood and His Merrie*

Men (1952), and Rob Roy in *Rob Roy, the Highlander Rogue* (1954), both Disney productions; Sir Walter Raleigh in *The Virgin Queen* (1956), with Bette Davis; and *Battle Hell* (1957), in which he played Lt. Cdr. John S. Kearns, RN, whose frigate, HMS *Amethyst,* was attacked by Chinese communists on the Yangtze River in April 1949.

In all, Todd made over forty films, including Alfred Hitchcock's *Stage Fright* (1950), with Marlene Dietrich, but by the early 1960s he seemed to lose interest in appearing in films, and he refocused his energy on his first love, the stage, leading to an eight-year run with the Mayfair Theatre in *The Business of Murder.* He co-formed Triumph Theatre Productions with two partners in 1970.

In 1987 Todd published the first volume of his memoirs, *Caught in the Act.*

★

Peter Ustinov

S creen and stage actor, film and stage director, playwright, novelist, and screenwriter, Peter Alexander Ustinov was born in London on 16 April 1921. He is the son of a journalist father of Russian descent, Iona Ustinov, and a French-born artist, Nadia Benois. His grandfather had been an officer in the Czar's Army. As a child he was a gifted mimic and could accurately imitate his parents and friends, much to their amusement. The headmaster at Westminster School in London, which he attended from 1934 to 1937, was less than amused.

Ustinov began studying acting under Michael St. Denis at the London Theatre Studio upon graduating from Westminster. He made his stage debut in a theater in Shere, Surrey, in 1938. During that period he began experimenting with writing plays. He wrote his first play,

(Photofest)

House of Regrets, in 1940 and made his film debut in *Hullo Fame* in 1941.

On 16 January 1942 Ustinov, following his call-up, signed his enlistment papers at Canterbury, Kent, and became Private Ustinov, #6411623, Royal Sussex Regiment. After basic training at Cliftonville on the southeast coast of England, he was put to work at a gun emplacement positioned on the cliffs of St. Margaret's Bay, Berkshire, guarding the beaches of Dover, "close enough for the Germans to lob shells."

The unit engaged in all types of maneuvers, and in his autobiography, *Dear Me,* Ustinov recalled one night exercise against the home guard in which he managed to capture the "enemy" headquarters, only to be ruled captured himself upon the arrival of a home guard umpire. Angered when they read his personal letters while searching him (they explained that they were simulating combat conditions), Ustinov decided to do some "simulating" of his own and spoke to his captors only in German. He managed to escape and ransack the headquarters, burning maps and wreaking havoc. Outraged, they reported Private Ustinov to his commanding officer, who only reluctantly supported him.

Having become aware of his background, the Army transferred the unruly soldier first to the Army Psychiatry Directorate in Troon, Scotland, then to the Army Kinematograph Service Unit (AKSU) in Wembley Park, London, where he was assigned to making morale films. Among those assigned to AKSU were the writer Eric Ambler, then a captain, and a director, Maj. Carol Reed. Ustinov, still a private, was assigned as a scriptwriter, but as an enlisted man he was still required to make the officers' tea and clean the latrines. He was sent to an Officer Selection Board but failed to pass the selection process.

Ustinov's first AKSU film was *The New Lot* (1943), about Army recruits, which was followed in 1944 by *The Way Ahead,* a tribute to the British "Tommy." The film was directed by Major Reed and starred Lt. Col. David Niven. The freedom of movement of British privates was somewhat restricted at the time. This policy had to be changed if Ustinov was to continue to work with officer actors in the production of AKSU films. The only conceivable reason for a private soldier to have any prolonged contact with an officer was if he were

Ustinov in his last American film, *Lorenzo's Oil* (1992). He enlisted in the British army in 1942 and was assigned to the Royal Sussex Regiment. He was later assigned to make morale films for the Army Kinematograph Service Unit, in Wembley Park, London, where he served primarily as a scriptwriter. After a stint with Supreme Headquarters, East Asian Forces, Ustinov was discharged in 1946. (Photofest)

appointed that officer's servant or "batman" (aide). Accordingly, Ustinov was assigned as Niven's batman. Niven gave Ustinov a pass that stated, "This man may go anywhere, and do anything at his discretion in the course of his duty." When stopped by military police, Ustinov would hand them his pass, and although they more or less resented seeing someone of his rank with such a waiver, they would let him go about his business. Despite this seemingly boundless freedom, he still had difficulty gaining admission to script conferences at the Ritz Hotel dressed in the uniform of an Army private.

Continuing to write plays, Ustinov produced two more in 1944, *House of Regrets* and *The Barnbury Nose,* both of which were successfully staged. Meanwhile, he volunteered for the commandos, but his request was denied. He was hospitalized for gallbladder complications and while there was diagnosed by a psychiatrist as being "mentally unfit" to make films, and it was suggested that he be transferred to the Ordnance Corps. Ustinov expressed his extreme displeasure to the psychiatrist, to the point of being arrested.

By now the Air Ministry was anxious to have a film of its own. Ustinov was selected to write and direct it: *The True Glory,* the story of the discovery of radar. The twenty-four-year-old private soon found himself in the company of Air Chief Marshal Sir Charles Portal and Air Marshal Sir Victor Tait inspecting troops at Malvern, where the film was being shot. Ustinov got many surprising looks from the cast and camera crew as the three toured the location.

Ustinov saw service in the Orient in an assignment to Supreme Headquarters, East Asian Forces. He was discharged from the British Army as a private in 1946 while he was filming *School for Secrets,* a training film starring Sir Ralph Richardson.

After his discharge Ustinov returned to the London theatrical scene, acting and writing. He directed his first film, *School of Secrets,* in 1946, and he continued to act in numerous films. He was first nominated for a Best Supporting Actor Oscar in 1951 for *Quo Vadis,* in which he played the Emperor Nero. He made his American stage debut in 1957 in *Romanoff and Juliet,* which he had written and produced in London the previous year. He won the Academy's Best Supporting Actor award in 1960 for his performance in *Spartacus* and won the award again in 1964 for *Topkapi.* He also was nominated for a Best Writing Oscar in 1969 for *Hot Millions.*

Ustinov has acted in, directed, or screen-written some seventy-five films. His last film appearance in an American movie was *Lorenzo's Oil* (1992). He has written twenty-seven books, numerous plays and articles, and a 1977 autobiography, *Dear Me.* He has received high acclaim for his television work, winning an Emmy Award in 1966 for *Barefoot in Athens* and a second Emmy in 1970 for *A Storm in Summer.* He was also awarded a Special Prize at the Berlin Festival in 1972.

He was made a Commander of the Order of the British Empire in 1975, was knighted by Queen Elizabeth in 1990, and has received several honorary degrees.

Oskar Werner

Noted for playing sensitive, vulnerable heroes, Oskar Werner was born Oskar Joseph Sschliessmayer in Vienna on 13 November 1922, the only child of Oskar and Stephanie Sschliessmayer. Raised by his mother after his parents divorced when he was six, Werner wanted to be an actor from the age of eleven. He performed in school productions and even appeared in an Austrian film while a student.

Upon finishing school in 1940, Werner applied to join the Burgtheater Repertory Company in Vienna. Amazingly, considering his lack of formal training, he was accepted. With the annexation of Austria by Nazi Germany in March 1938, Austrian males were subject to conscription into the German Armed Forces, and in 1941 Werner was drafted into the Wehrmacht (German Army) and assigned to an

(Photofest)

artillery battery. Less than enthusiastic at the prospect of dying for the Führer, he was able to avoid being sent to the front lines, instead serving in garrison duty outside Vienna while continuing to perform at the Burgtheater. In 1944 the theater was closed by order of the propaganda minister, Josef Goebbels, and Werner, now a *Gefreiter* (corporal), was sent for officers' training. After only two weeks he was returned to his unit as "unsuitable" for such training.

As the bombing of Germany intensified toward the end of the war, Werner was wounded in an American bombing raid and was sent to a military hospital to recover. Upon his release he deserted rather than return to his unit and spent the last three months of the war hiding in the woods, risking capture and immediate execution by SS squads hunting deserters.

He traveled to Vienna after the German surrender and returned to the theater, making regular appearances at the Salzburg Festival. At the same time he began to appear in films across Europe and in England, and he was beginning to be noticed in the United States.

Werner's American debut occurred when he was offered the part of an anti-Nazi German POW in Anatole Litvak's film *Decision before Dawn* (1951), based on George Howe's novel *Call It Treason.* The film was a critical success and earned such favorable reviews for Werner that he was offered a contract with 20th Century Fox. He came to Hollywood in 1952, but his career never developed. He was released from his contract and returned to Europe.

Werner acted in the German film *Der Letzte Akt* (1956), which was released in the United States as *The Last Ten Days of Hitler,* and the French film *Jules et Jim* (1961) before being nominated for an Oscar as Best Actor in Stanley Kramer's *Ship of Fools* (1965), in which he played the ship's doctor. Later films include *Fahrenheit 451* (1966), *The Shoes of the Fisherman* (1968), and *Voyage of the Damned* (1976). He died in Marburg, West Germany, on 23 October 1984.

★

PART 2

Others Who Served

★

Others Who Served: An Alphabetical Listing

Harry Baur

A French stage and screen actor who mostly appeared in character roles, Harry Baur was one of the most popular cinema actors in France in the 1930s. In 1942 his Jewish wife was arrested. He was also taken into custody by the Nazis in Berlin that same year for forging an *Ahnpass*, a certificate of "Aryan" ancestry. He was sent to prison and tortured by the Gestapo. Released in April 1943, he died a few days later under suspicious circumstances.

Notable films: *Les Misérables* (1934), *The Life and Loves of Beethoven* (1935), *Rasputin* (1937).

Rossano Brazzi

Internationally popular Italian screen actor Rossano Brazzi is best remembered for his romantic film performances. Probably one of Italy's busiest actors, he appeared in over two hundred films from the 1940s through the early 1980s. Although he appeared in such American-made movies as *Three Coins in the Fountain* (1954), *The Barefoot Contessa* (1954), and *South Pacific* (1958), Brazzi never achieved significant stardom outside of Italy.

During World War II, Brazzi, whose father was strongly antifascist, joined resistance groups that helped supply food for escaped Allied POWs.

Yul Brynner

Best known for his performance in *The King and I,* Yul Brynner was born Taidje Kahn on Sakhalin island in northern Japan in 1915 and became a citizen of Switzerland in 1960. In 1956 he won the Best Actor Oscar for the movie version of the stage play. In 1985 he was awarded a Special Tony for his stage performance in a revival of the show. Early in his career he was an acrobat in a French circus and toured Europe and the United States with a Shakespearean troupe. During World War II (1942 to D-Day), he worked as a French-speaking radio announcer and commentator for the U.S. Office of War Information broadcasting propaganda to occupied France. Following the war he worked mostly in films and on the stage. He also did some directing and television work. He died of lung cancer in 1985.

Notable films: *The Ten Commandments* (1956), *Anastasia* (1956), *The Brothers Karamazov* (1958), *Solomon and Sheba* (1959), *The Magnificent Seven* (1960), *Futureworld* (1976).

Noel Coward

One of the most creative men of the arts of the twentieth century, British-born Noel Coward was called before the Army Examining Board in January 1918. The young man—he was nineteen at the time—had no desire to serve in the military, saw no glory in war, and was ill prepared for Army discipline. Inducted into the Army, Coward was attached to the Artists Light Rifles at Essex. Plagued by headaches and insomnia, he spent the majority of his nine and a half months' service at the First London General Hospital in Camberwell and the General Military Hospital in Colchester. At Colchester a medical board ordered Coward returned to full duty, but he consulted with another medical officer who determined him to be unfit for duty and arranged for him to be given a medical discharge.

Returning to the theater, Coward went on to write fifty plays, including *Private Lives* (1930) and *Blithe Spirit* (1941); to compose over one hundred songs, including "Some Day I'll Find You" and "Mad Dogs and Englishmen"; and to make films such as *In Which We Serve* (1942) and *Brief Encounter* (1946). He was a lyricist and a playwright and wrote two volumes of short stories as well as novels, including *To Step Aside* (1939), *Star Quality* (1951), and *Our Man in Havana* (1960). Noel Coward died in Jamaica in 1973.

Leo Genn

A graduate of Cambridge and a practicing barrister when he made his stage debut in 1930, Leo Genn was able to continue with his practice while gaining experience on the stage and silver screen. He served with the Royal Artillery during World War II, was promoted to lieutenant colonel in 1943, and was awarded the croix de guerre at the end of the European war. He next joined a British team that investigated war crimes at the Bergen-Belsen concentration camp and later became an assistant prosecutor at the Bergen-Belsen trial proceedings. During his forty-year theatrical career he appeared in over fifty films. In 1951 he was nominated as Best Supporting Actor for his performance in the epic *Quo Vadis*.

Notable films: *Moby Dick* (1956), with Gregory Peck; *The Longest Day* (1962), with John Wayne; *Fifty-five Days at Peking* (1963), with Charlton Heston.

Lorne Greene

Lorne Greene made his television debut in 1953 playing Big Brother in a live performance of George Orwell's *1984* on CBS's highly rated program *Studio One*. He made his film debut playing the Apostle Peter in *The Silver Chalice* (1954). His last role would be portraying Gen. Sam Houston in the 1987 television movie *Thirteen Days to Glory*. But there is only one role for which Lorne Greene will forever be remembered, and that was Ben Cartwright, patriarch of the Cartwright family on the Ponderosa ranch on television's *Bonanza*. A pioneer in family values, *Bonanza* dominated Sunday nights for fourteen years (1959–73) as "Pa" Cartwright dispensed fatherly wisdom to Adam, Hoss, and Little Joe.

Lorne Hyman Greene was born on 12 February 1915 to Russian-Jewish immigrants in Ottawa, Ontario, Canada. He attended Queens University in Kingston (1932–37), studying chemical engineering until enticed away by the Drama Guild. He remained there producing, directing, and acting in plays and later accepted a fellowship to the Neighborhood Playhouse School of Theater in New York City, where he studied for two years.

In 1939, with the outbreak of World War II, Greene obtained work at the Canadian Broadcasting Corporation, where he rose to the position of chief radio announcer. The early news from the war was less than encouraging, and Greene's somber voice detailing the setbacks earned him the sobriquet "the Voice of Doom."

Greene also served as narrator in a number of wartime films, including *War Clouds in the Pacific* (1941), *Churchill's Islands* (1941), and *Inside Fighting China* (1942). In 1942 he entered military service, but accounts differ as to whether he served as a private in the Canadian Army, doing home-front interviews, or as a flying officer in the Royal Canadian Air Force. In any event, he was out of uniform by 1945.

Legend has it that Greene's performance in a 1957 episode of the television series *Wagon Train* led to his selection for the role of Cartwright, a part for which he was ideally suited. His performances in other television programs such as *Griff* (1973–74), *Battlestar Galactica* (1978–79), and *Code Red* (1981–82) would never approach his *Bonanza* status.

Lorne Greene died in Santa Monica, California, in 1987.

Louis Jourdan

French actor and twenty-six-year veteran of stage, screen, and television, Louis Jourdan tried to enlist when Germany invaded Poland but was underage. France subsequently fell to German *blitzkrieg* forces, and Jourdan was put on a work gang where he cut wood, dug ditches, and helped build roads. He was ordered to appear in propaganda films for the Nazis; however, he escaped to join his parents near Cannes. He later carried messages for the French underground.

Notable films: *Letter from an Unknown Woman* (1948), *The Paradine Case* (1948), *Madame Bovary* (1949), *Three Coins in the Fountain* (1954), *Gigi* (1958), *Can Can* (1960).

Paul Lukas

Stage and screen actor Paul Lukas was born in Budapest, Hungary, on 26 May 1894. His father had hoped that, after completing his education at the College of Budapest, he would join the family's highly successful advertising business; however, since childhood Lukas had wanted to be an actor. Before a decision could be made, Europe became embroiled in World War I. Lukas, though underage, volunteered for a year's military service. In 1915 the young soldier found himself facing Russian soldiers on Hungary's eastern border. He was severely wounded, eventually found to be unfit for duty, and subsequently released from the Army.

Following his discharge he entered the Actor's School of the National Theater in Budapest and made his stage debut in 1916. He worked next with the Opera House Company in the Hungarian town of Kassa and then in 1918 joined the Comedy Theater in Budapest, where he remained for seven years, appearing in some sixty productions. In the years that followed he performed in numerous Hungarian films and plays and achieved matinee-idol status. In 1928 he made his first film in the United States, playing opposite actress Pola Negri in *The Woman from Moscow*. During the remainder of his career he appeared in over fifty films in the United States and England. His greatest performance on stage and film was in Lillian Hellman's *Watch on the Rhine*. His stage rendition in 1941 won him the Delia Austrian Medal of the Drama League for the most distinguished performance of the year. He won a Best Actor Oscar and the New York Film Critics Award in 1943 for repeating his performance in the film version.

Notable films: *Twenty Thousand Leagues under the Sea* (1954), with Kirk Douglas; *Tender Is the Night* (1962), with Jason Robards; *Lord Jim* (1965), with Peter O'Toole.

Herbert Marshall

Urbane and suave, Herbert Marshall played the lead in numerous sophisticated comedies in the 1930s and 1940s. Born Herbert Bough Falcon Marshall in London on 23 May 1890, he worked for a time as an accountant before taking to the London stage.

With the outbreak of World War I, Marshall enlisted in the 14th London Scots Regiment of the British Army. Ronald Colman also enlisted in the same regiment, but it is unknown if the two men were acquaintances. Among the first British troops shipped overseas to France, Marshall saw heavy combat and was severely wounded in 1915, resulting in the loss of his right leg. He was cited for bravery and evacuated to a military hospital in England, where he would spend the next thirteen months. Leaving the Army, Marshall returned to acting, where he felt that his limp gave him a "jaunty" air, but nonetheless he kept the loss of his leg a secret for most of his career.

Marshall made his screen debut in *Mumsie* (1927). *The List of Adrian Messenger* (1963) was the last film he completed before his death in Beverly Hills, California, on 22 January 1966.

Notable films: *The Razor's Edge* (1946), with Tyrone Power; *The Secret Garden* (1949); *The Virgin Queen* (1955), with Bette Davis.

Raymond Massey

Because of his exceptional portrayal of the president in the film *Abe Lincoln in Illinois* (1940), Canadian-born actor Raymond Massey was known as "the man who took the face of Lincoln off the penny and put it into the hearts of millions of Americans." At the start of World War I he enrolled in the Canadian Officers Training Corps at the University of Toronto and was commissioned a second lieutenant in 1915 in the Canadian Field Artillery. He was sent to France in 1916 and was wounded that same year at Ypres. Upon his recovery he served with the British Military Mission to the United States, instructing gunnery at Yale and Princeton universities. The last year of the war, 1918, he was assigned to the British Expeditionary Force in Siberia.

Thunder and lightning were synonymous with this actor with the booming, authoritative voice, the grand manner, and the tall, broad-shouldered build of a person born to command. He used these assets with great skill throughout his acting career.

Notable films: *The Fountainhead* (1949), *East of Eden* (1955), *Prince of Players* (1955).

Marcello Mastroianni

One of Italy's most popular actors, Marcello Mastroianni attained international stardom in the movie *La Dolce Vita* (1960), a controversial film in which he played a society reporter who is drawn into a circle of wealthy, decadent people who indulge themselves in the "sweet life." His co-star, the beautiful, sultry actress Anita Ekberg, also gained stardom for her performance in the movie. Mastroianni appeared in over one hundred films, mostly Italian, during his fifty-year career. He is best remembered by American moviegoers for his performances in *Divorce Italian Style* (1961); *Yesterday, Today, and Tomorrow* (1961), co-starring Sophia Loren; and *8 1/2* (1963). He earned three U.S. Academy Award nominations and numerous foreign film acting awards.

Mastroianni was born on 28 September 1924 in Fontana, Italy, the son of a carpenter. After completing school he worked in his father's carpentry shop in Rome. When Italy joined the Axis powers during World War II, he found himself drawing maps for the Germans. When talking about the war in later years Mastroianni said that it had all been simply stupid; they were still drawing maps of Sicily when the Americans were in Florence. He was eventually sent to a forced labor camp in the Italian Alps. He escaped to Venice, where he made a meager living painting pictures for tourists.

Mastroianni died in 1996.

Ray Milland

In 1925, at the age of eighteen, Ray Milland traveled to Newport, South Wales, where he presented himself to the commanding officer of the South Wales Borderers. It was his intention, he announced, to enlist in the Household Cavalry, known as "the Blues." An interview was arranged, and within a week he reported to the Household Guards depot in Albany Street, London, where he was given a comprehensive interview and physical exam.

Accepted, he enlisted for a term of four years' active duty and eight years' reserve, a decision he would later recall as "wise." Allotted horse "B-63," Milland spent the next eight weeks training in the use of saber, lance, sword, and rifle, all while mounted. "Passed out" as a Household Cavalryman, Milland was assigned to B Squadron, B Troop, where he continued training in marksmanship, horsemanship, signals, fencing, and boxing. An expert shot, he became a member of his company's rifle team and won many prestigious competitions, including the Risley Match in England. He was at some point assigned mounted guard duty at Whitehall but disliked "sitting like an equestrian statue."

When his four-year active-duty service was completed, Milland, attracted to the theater, tried his hand at acting. He was discovered by a Hollywood talent scout while performing on the stage in London, came to America, and signed with Paramount Pictures. When World War II began, he tried to enlist in the U.S. Army Air Forces but was rejected because of an impaired left hand. He worked as a civilian flight instructor for the Army and toured with a United Service Organizations (USO) troupe in the South Pacific in 1944.

Notable films: *The Lost Weekend* (1945), for which he won an Oscar as Best Actor; *Golden Earrings* (1947); *The Big Clock* (1948); *Dial M for Murder* (1954); *Aces High* (1976).

John Mills

One of Britain's leading screen stars during World War II, John Mills first tried to enlist in the Royal Navy at the age of thirty but was told that enlistment quotas were filled and no more personnel were needed at the time. He subsequently saw a poster that blared out, "Join the Engineers," which he did. He completed his basic training and was posted as a sapper to the 346 Company (a searchlight unit) at Royston, Hertfordshire. In September 1940 he was ordered to officer cadet training at Shrivenham, Wiltshire. He was commissioned a second lieutenant and posted to the 1st Rifle Battalion Monmouth Regiment at Trowbridge, Wiltshire, commanding a dozen sites near Trowbridge. A few weeks after his posting he was taken to a Bath hospital with severe stomach pains. Diagnosed as having a duodenal ulcer, he was declared unfit for service and discharged in December 1940.

Mills won an Oscar in 1970 for his portrayal of the village idiot in *Ryan's Daughter*. He performed in over ninety films and was knighted in 1977. In January 2001 Sir John, at the age of ninety-two, walked down the aisle at St. Mary's Church in Denham to renew his wedding vows with his wife of sixty years, Mary. He had been denied a church service when they first married because he was serving in the Army during the war. They had been forced to marry at London's Marylebone Register Office while he was on a forty-eight-hour pass. The renewal ceremony was attended by one hundred friends and family members, and Britain's queen mother sent a congratulatory telegram. Sir John is the father of actresses Juliet and Haley Mills.

Notable films: *The Chalk Garden* (1963), *Young Winston* (1972), *The Big Sleep* (1978), *Gandhi* (1982), *Sahara* (1984), *Hamlet* (1996).

Leslie Nielsen

Noted for his deadpan delivery of absurd dialogue in farcical comedies, Leslie Nielsen was born in Regina, Saskatchewan, Canada, on 11 February 1926. His father, a "Mountie" with the Royal Canadian Mounted Police, was a strict disciplinarian, and Nielsen credits his acting ability to his need to lie to his father to avoid being punished.

He left home during World War II at the age of seventeen to enlist in the Royal Canadian Air Force. He was accepted for pilot training and learned to fly in the British-made Cornell, a single-engine trainer. It appears that he served overseas, but his only statement on his service was that he "cheered up pilots going on missions."

After the war, Nielsen attended Lorne Greene's Academy of Radio Arts in Toronto, the Neighborhood Playhouse in New York City, then the Actors Studio, before beginning to act on television and in films. His early serious performances include *Forbidden Planet* (1956), co-starring "Robby the Robot"; *Tammy and the Bachelor* (1957), playing Debbie Reynolds's love interest; and his starring role as Revolutionary War hero Francis Marion in Walt Disney's television series *Swamp Fox* (1959–61). His other ventures into television included starring roles in such series as *The New Breed* (1961–62), *Peyton Place* (1965), *Bracken's World* (1969), *The Protectors* (1969–70), and *Police Squad* (1982), as well as many made-for-TV movies.

Nielsen's later screwball film comedies include *Airplane* (1980), *The Naked Gun: From the Files of Police Squad* (1988), *The Naked Gun 2¹/₂: The Smell of Fear* (1991), and *The Naked Gun 33¹/₃: The Final Insult* (1994), as well as farces like *Dracula, Dead and Loving It* (1995) and *Wrongfully Accused* (1998).

John Schlesinger

Although primarily a film director, John Schlesinger appeared in several movies during his early theatrical career. He enlisted in the British Army in 1943 and was assigned to the Royal Engineers as an architectural draftsman. He recalls that he was not a great soldier—"too much of a rebel." After training in the north of England, he was sent to Singapore, but his assignment seemed to consist primarily of designing latrines. As Schlesinger related in an interview, "That's all I seemed to do. I was the shithouse designer for this unit. I thought this is a mug's game, to hell with it." He was discharged from the Army as a lance corporal in 1947.

Notable films (as a director): *Far from the Madding Crowd* (1967); *Midnight Cowboy* (1969), for which he won an Oscar for Best Director; *Sunday, Bloody Sunday* (1971); *Marathon Man* (1976); *The Falcon and the Snowman* (1985).

Arnold Schwarzenegger

Arnold Schwarzenegger was born in Graz, Austria, on 30 July 1947. Upon graduation from secondary school he enlisted in the Austrian army, which allowed him time to pursue his bent for body building. He spent a year in the military and later said, "For me the Army was a good experience. I liked regimentation, the firm, rigid structure. The whole idea of uniforms and medals appealed to me."

After his discharge Schwarzenegger managed a health and body-building club in Munich, and it was there that he developed perhaps the world's most perfect male physique. He won the Mr. World title five times and was named Mr. Olympia six times. He came to the United States at the invitation of Weider Enterprises, publisher of the magazines *Muscle Builder* and *Mr. America.* In addition to his body-building interest, he dreamed of becoming an actor. In 1976 he landed a role in the film *Stay Hungry* and won a Golden Globe award for Best New Actor. The rest is history, for Schwarzenegger went on to win fame and fortune in the movie industry.

Notable films: *Pumping Iron* (1977), *Conan the Barbarian* (1982), *The Terminator* (1984), *Total Recall* (1990), *True Lies* (1994).

Peter Sellers

Born in Southsea, Hampshire, England, on 8 September 1925, to a musician father and an actress mother, with numerous other relatives in show business, Peter Sellers first performed with his parents at age five.

A poor student in college, Sellers was working as a drummer in a dance band in 1943 when he entered the Royal Air Force (RAF). He was sent to Cardington-Bedfordshire, where he was assigned the duties of an armorer assistant, responsible for loading ammunition into the wing guns of squadron planes. He entertained the men in his unit with stories and impressions of their officers. His talent was recognized, and he was assigned to an RAF entertainment troop, the Ralph Reader Gang Show, which traveled throughout the Middle East area of operations putting on shows. He was discharged as a corporal in 1946 and returned to England.

Sellers returned to a career in vaudeville, radio, and later motion pictures. His breakthrough role was a three-character performance in *The Mouse That Roared* (1959), but he is best remembered as bumbling Inspector Clouseau in *The Pink Panther* (1959) and its sequels and as Group Capt. Lionel Mandrake, President Merkin Muffley, and the title character in *Dr. Strangelove* (1964). Sellers died in London on 24 July 1980.

Jacques Sernas

A noted international actor, Jacques Sernas was born in Lithuania in 1925, was educated in Paris, and enjoyed a successful screen career playing mostly in French-and Italian-produced films. During World War II he joined the French resistance and was captured by the Germans and imprisoned in Buchenwald. Following the end of the war he enrolled in medical school, but he soon dropped out and went into acting. He made his screen debut in 1946.

Notable films: *Helen of Troy* (1956), with Brigitte Bardot; *La Dolce Vita* (1960), with Anita Ekberg; *Midas Run* (1969).

William Travers

British actor William Travers was born in Newcastle-upon-Tyne on 3 January 1922. A tall, muscular leading man, he was most at home performing in films with outdoor settings. He married Virginia McKenna with whom he co-starred in the movie *Born Free* (1966), the story of two Kenya game wardens who raise a pet lioness, Elsa. The film won two Oscars. During World War II, Travers was in the British Army serving in the Pacific. While engaging Japanese soldiers he was severely wounded and escaped capture by losing his pursuers in the jungle.

Notable films: *Bhowani Junction* (1956), *The Barretts of Wimpole Street* (1957), *Duel at Diablo* (1966).

★

PART 3

Entertainers

★

Annabella

Marine Transport Squadron 353 was based on the Pacific island of Saipan in 1944 toward the end of World War II. The squadron was equipped with C-46 Curtiss Commando transport aircraft, used to haul supplies and carry out casualties from Iwo Jima and Okinawa. One of the planes carried the words "Blithe Spirit" on its nose section under the cockpit. The commander of that plane was Marine 1st Lt. Tyrone Power, famed American actor and husband of French-born actress Annabella. While Power flew transport missions in the Pacific, his wife was entertaining Allied troops in Europe as the leading lady in Noel Coward's play *Blithe Spirit*.

Annabella, a blonde film beauty of the 1930s, was born Suzanne Georgette Charpentier in 1909 in Paris. She changed her name to just Annabella after reading Edgar Allan Poe's "Annabel Lee." She began

(Photofest)

her film career in 1930 in France and made movies in Hungary, Germany, and Austria. By the late 1930s she had become one of the most sought after leading ladies in continental filmmaking. Her appearance in the first color film ever made in England, *Wings of Glory* (1937), which co-starred Henry Fonda, caught the attention of Hollywood filmmakers, and she was put under contract by 20th Century Fox.

For the next several years she appeared in numerous American movies playing opposite such stars as Charles Boyer, Paul Lukas, William Powell, Robert Young, and Tyrone Power, whom she married in 1939. During the 1940s she appeared on Broadway in productions of *Blithe Spirit, Jacobowsky and the Colonel,* and Jean-Paul Sartre's play *No Exit,* which was directed by John Huston and co-starred Claude Dauphin. In 1947 she appeared opposite James Cagney in *13 Rue Madeleine.*

With the liberation of Paris in August 1944, Annabella, anxious to see her family again, joined the United Service Organizations, cast as the star of *Blithe Spirit.* While entertaining in Italy she was cleared to fly aboard a military aircraft going to Paris, where she was finally reunited with her family. She spent a few weeks with them before catching up with her *Blithe Spirit* company, which itself was unsuccessfully chasing Gen. George Patton's Third Army as it sped through France toward the German border. The Powers were divorced in 1948. Annabella later married actor Oskar Werner, but they were divorced in 1971.

Annabella returned to France to care for her mother, and she often lamented that she had to give up her American citizenship, taken out in 1942. During her retirement years she was a volunteer worker for prison welfare in France. She divided her time between her Paris apartment and her twenty-six-acre farm in the French Pyrenees, where she pastured sheep. Annabella died in 1996 at the age of eighty-six at her home in Neuilly-sur-Seine, a suburb of Paris. She is survived by a daughter, Anne Werner Power.

Josephine Baker

American expatriate Josephine Baker gained legendary fame as a
singer and dancer in Paris during the 1920s and 1930s. She
appeared in numerous French films, was featured in revues
at all of the Parisian cafes and clubs, and was a regular main attrac-
tion at the Folies Bergère. In addition, she made numerous tours in
Europe and South America.

When Belgium was invaded by the Germans in 1940, she became a
Red Cross volunteer, attending to refugees escaping to France. After Germany invaded France in June 1940, she joined the French underground
network in Paris and was particularly successful in obtaining critical
intelligence from an attaché in the Italian embassy, which she passed
on to Jacques Abtey, a French Army intelligence officer. In 1942 she
entertained Allied troops in North Africa and the Middle East as a sub-

(Photofest)

lieutenant in the Women's Auxiliary of the Free French forces. For her services rendered during the war she was decorated with the Legion of Honor and the Rosette of the Resistance by the French government.

Josephine Baker was born on 3 June 1906, the daughter of a washerwoman. She started entertaining at the age of eight, singing in Harlem nightclubs, and then became an exuberant Broadway chorine before going on to Paris, where she found fame and fortune. During her peak years in France she was the highest-paid entertainer in Europe. Baker became a French citizen in 1937; she was married twice, to French industrialist Jean Lyon in 1940 (the union ended in annulment) and to French orchestra leader Jo Bouillon in 1947.

There was much more to Baker than her act; she became a role model for young black women. In 1951 the National Association for the Advancement of Colored People dedicated a Josephine Baker Day, celebrated in Harlem in recognition of her work for racial equality, work that was typified by her adoption of twelve orphans of mixed colors and creeds. In 1964 she faced losing her estate in southern France because of sizable debts but was rescued by Prince Rainier and Princess Grace of Monaco. Later she returned to the stage and thrilled audiences around the world with an exciting new revue.

Josephine Baker died from a stroke in 1975. As a decorated war hero she was accorded a full-scale military funeral at the Madeleine, with a flag-draped coffin and a twenty-one-gun salute. She was buried in Monaco.

Madeleine Carroll

Described by stage and film critics as looking "the way every blonde should look" and "as fragile and feminine as a Dresden shepherdess," Madeleine Carroll was the first British actress to become a motion picture star in both England and America. During her long theatrical career she performed on stage and in films (making over forty motion pictures) and appeared on a number of radio programs and television shows.

Madeleine Carroll was born on 26 February 1909, in West Bromwich, Staffordshire, England. Her father was of Irish descent, and her mother was a native of France. She was christened Marie-Madeleine but later changed her name to Madeleine. She had one sister, Marguerite, who was killed at the age of nineteen during a German air raid on London in 1940. Carroll was educated in local public

(Photofest)

schools, where she majored in French. Her secondary interest was in international affairs. Though she showed a bent for dramatics and was encouraged to study theater, she went on to receive a Bachelor of Arts degree with honors and a postgraduate degree in Paris. She later accepted a teaching position at a girls' school in Hove near Brighton, England, where she taught French, and she also tutored students in Birmingham. With the wages she earned from these teaching positions she was able to go to London and seek a career on the stage.

Carroll began her theatrical career in 1927 with a small part in a play at the Winter Garden Theatre. Other parts came her way, and she joined several touring companies, gaining needed experience. Finally she was selected from 150 applicants to play the leading role in *The Guns of Loos* (1928), a British World War I film. Her next picture, *The First Born* (1929), began to win her a popular following.

For the next several years she traveled between the United States and England appearing in plays and motion pictures in both countries. One important film she made in the United States at the time was *The Thirty-nine Steps* (1935), which was directed by Alfred Hitchcock and co-starred Robert Donat (star of *Goodbye Mr. Chips* [1935], for which he won a Best Actor Oscar). This film brought her to the attention of American audiences. Carroll subsequently appeared in numerous theater productions and motion pictures until America entered World War II.

By that time Carroll was one of the most popular international stars in the business. But she had never forgotten the loss of her sister, saying, "The personal loss drove home the full meaning of the hideous fate that had closed in on the people of Europe." Fulfilling all her contracts in 1941, she ended her professional appearances to accept the unsalaried post of entertainment director of the United Seamen's Service in New York City. She remained at this post for the next eighteen months, organizing various benefits and entertainment programs for the seamen, whom she considered to be the "forgotten warriors" of the war.

Carroll joined the Red Cross as a hospital worker in 1943 and a year later was assigned to the 17th General Hospital in Naples, where she tended to the wounded from the Monte Cassino and Anzio campaigns. She next was ordered to the 61st Station Hospital in Foggia,

Italy, and after a year with the 61st worked in hospital trains that carried wounded soldiers to hospitals in French cities. Following the end of the war she aided in the rehabilitation of those returning from concentration camps.

During the late 1940s Carroll returned to the American screen, where she made a few nondescript movies, but she triumphed in 1948 with her Broadway stage performance in Fay Kanin's *Goodbye, My Fancy.*

In recognition of her wartime service she was given the Legion of Honor by the French government and the Medal of Freedom, the highest award given by the U.S. Army to civilians.

Carroll was married and divorced four times; American movie actor Sterling Hayden was her second husband, French film producer-director Henri Lavorel was her third, and *Life* magazine publisher Andrew Heiskell was her fourth. She died in 1989 in Marbella, Spain, which had been her home for more than fifteen years.

Marlene Dietrich

I n 1970, Marlene Dietrich was named the world's most glamorous grandmother. The sixty-six-year-old stage and film star still possessed the bewitching magic that had made her a legend since her appearance in small roles in German films in the 1920s. She was a beautiful woman with a low, sultry voice, a figure envied by other women and appreciated by men throughout most of her life, a sleepy, mocking manner, and a strangely angelic yet exotic face, with penciled eyebrows.

She was born Maria Magdalene von Losch in Berlin in 1904. Edouard von Losch, a cavalry lieutenant, was her stepfather. Her real father, Louis Erich Otto Dietrich, an officer in the Royal Prussian Police, died when she was a child, killed on the Russian front at the end of World War I. She was brought up in a conservative middle-class home

Marlene Dietrich chatting with five members of the U.S. Women's Army Auxiliary Corps (WACs) somewhere in France. Dietrich became an American citizen in 1939 and during World War II she traveled all over the world entertaining Allied troops. For her services, she received the Medal of Freedom, the highest award given by the U.S. Army to a civilian. In 1951 she received the French Legion of Honor. (Photofest)

and in her teens studied violin, hoping to become a concert violinist. She gave up this dream, however, after injuring her wrist and turned to the stage. During the 1920s she appeared in numerous movie roles in Germany, eventually being selected to play leads in films that brought her such popularity that German film critics began to compare her to Greta Garbo and Elisabeth Bergner. She was eventually discovered by American film director Josef von Sternberg and cast as the lead in the German film *The Blue Angel* (1930). Her performance in the movie led to international stardom, and she soon went to Hollywood, where she was transformed into a glamorous woman of mystery. After appearing in several films directed by von Sternberg, she became a legend.

While back in England in 1937 to appear in the film *Knight without Armour,* she was approached by Nazi agents who tried to tempt her into returning to Germany to appear in German movies. In fact, she was visited by Germany's ambassador to England, Joachim von Ribbentrop, with a personal invitation from Hitler. She showed the ambassador the door, and as a result her films were banned in Germany.

Dietrich became a U.S. citizen in 1939, and during World War II she devoted an enormous amount of time to traveling to the far reaches of the world entertaining Allied troops. She stated that her three years of wartime work entertaining American soldiers from Anzio to the Aleutians was the only important thing she had ever done. In many cases she paid her own way to be with the troops. Bundled in a GI overcoat, standing in chow lines and sleeping in dugouts, Dietrich put on a performance that was a triumph of stamina. She sang songs from her old movies and did some mind-reading tricks. As she said, "It wasn't too hard to read a GI's mind overseas." When the Allied troops landed in France, she was onstage at Anzio and was given the privilege of announcing the invasion to her GI audience. She sang for captured German soldiers and was surprised that the POWs showed her no bitterness, since she was widely known to be anti-Nazi. When she sang the songs from *The Blue Angel,* the soldiers looked at her adoringly.

During the war the U.S. Treasury Department awarded Dietrich a special citation for her successful selling of war bonds. Following the end of the war she received the Medal of Freedom from the U.S. Army for her "extraordinary record in entertaining troops overseas." In 1951, in recognition of her services to France during the war, she was presented with the French Legion of Honor by Henri Bonnet, the French ambassador to the United States.

In the 1950s Dietrich entered a new phase in her career, singing in cabarets and recording many of her most popular songs. She packed theaters in London, Paris, Moscow, Las Vegas, and New York. She continued to be popular through the early 1970s but retired from show business shortly thereafter. Her last performance was in a screen biography of herself, *Marlene* (1984), produced by Maximilian Schell, in which she is heard on tape but never seen.

Marlene Dietrich died in 1992.

★

Jessica Dragonette

Jessica Dragonette was perhaps one of the most popular singers of the twentieth century. During the 1930s and 1940s she was heard on NBC radio by sixty-six million Americans weekly. The gifted soprano was so endeared to the public that she was often called "the Star of Stars," "the Princess of Song," "the Sweetheart of the Air," and "the Queen of Radio."

Jessica Dragonette was born on 14 February 1900 in Calcutta, India, and brought to America when she was just a child. She was subsequently orphaned and placed in a convent, where she was raised by nuns. She studied voice at the Georgian Court Convent and College in Lakewood, New Jersey, and in 1924 she won a job as an unseen angel in the choir of impresario Max Reinhardt's production of the Broadway musical *The Miracle*. She next appeared on stage in *The Student*

(Photofest)

Prince and later played the lead role in *The Grand Street Follies*.

Dragonette then left the stage and for the next twenty-two years performed on radio, bringing operetta and semiclassical music to Americans across the nation. She began her radio career in 1926 in a musical-comedy hour. She next appeared in *The Coca-Cola Girl,* radio's first original singing/acting serial, as Vivian. She sang on *The Philco Hour* from 1927 to 1930; in the *Cities Service* concert series from 1930 to 1937; on the *Ford Summer Show* in 1940; and was the star of the CBS network's *Saturday Night Serenade* in 1940. She was also among the many stars who were heard on the first radio broadcast from the NBC studios when Radio City was opened in New York on 11 November 1932.

No other radio star did more to support the World War II war effort than Jessica Dragonette. She performed at countless war bond rallies and toured military bases and camps entertaining troops throughout the war. For her tireless service she was awarded a United Service Organizations Camp Shows Commendation, the U.S. Treasury Silver Medal, and Wings from both the Army and Navy. She was given the honorary rank of colonel in the U.S. Army Air Forces.

Dragonette's movie career was short. She appeared in the movie *The Big Broadcast* (1936) and was the singing voice of Princess Glory in *Gulliver's Travels* (1939). Her true home was the concert stage, where her performances drew thousands of fans. Over 150,000 people once crowded into Grant Park in Chicago to hear her. In Minneapolis, fifteen thousand attended a single performance despite a blizzard and a transportation strike; eighteen thousand heard her at the Potomac Water Gate in Washington, D.C.; and she drew an audience of twenty-two thousand when she sang with the Philharmonic Symphony Orchestra at New York's Lewisohn Stadium.

Following the end of World War II, Jessica Dragonette married Nicholas Meredith Turner, a New York contractor. In 1952, in recognition of her promotion of Spanish music, she was presented with the Medal of the Knot of the Order of Isabella the Catholic by the Spanish ambassador to the United States. A devout Roman Catholic throughout her life, she was invested as a Lady of the Grand Cross of the Equestrian Order of the Holy Sepulchre of Jerusalem and was awarded the Pro Pontifice et Ecclesia Cross from the Vatican for her contribution to music.

Jessica Dragonette continued to sing on television specials and make guest appearances on NBC until her death on 18 March 1980, at the age of seventy.

★

Vera Lynn

usic in many respects becomes a part of every war. Songs with lyrics that speak of love, loneliness, and the joy of reunion become part of the soul of nations whose sons and daughters have gone off to war. These songs endure. Even today the melodies of World War II continue to be played, bringing back memories never to be forgotten.

Entertainers who traveled to far-off battlefields brought a touch of home to those fighting the war. Some of those songs will be forever associated with certain vocalists: Jo Stafford will be remembered for her rendition of "I'll Be Seeing You," the Andrews Sisters for "Boogie Woogie Bugle Boy," Helen Forrest for "I'll Walk Alone," and British songstress Vera Lynn for "We'll Meet Again" and "The White Cliffs of Dover," just to mention a few. There were other entertainers who raised the morale of the troops during World War I, Korea, and Vietnam, but the music of World War II in particular seemed to cap-

(Photofest)

ture the hearts of people all over the world.

During World War II most American entertainers traveled under the auspices of the United Service Organizations (USO). When the war broke out in Europe, the Theatre Royal, Drury Lane, became the headquarters of the Entertainments National Service Association (ENSA). This organization was similar to the American USO, and entertainment units were organized and rehearsed in the Theatre Royal and then dispatched to play their vital morale-boosting role in Britain's war effort. The most popular British singer of World War II was Vera Lynn, whose "We'll Meet Again" became almost a national anthem.

Vera Lynn was born in London's East End in 1917 and began her singing career at the age of seven. At fifteen she became a vocalist with Howard Baker's Orchestra, and in 1935 she made her first radio broadcast with the Joe Loss Orchestra and then was hired by Charlie Kunz. She became the leading British singer of the war years, hosting a BBC radio program, *Sincerely Yours*.

In early 1944 Vera Lynn joined ENSA and, dressed in her ENSA uniform, volunteered for a foreign tour to entertain troops. She selected the British Fourteenth Army ("the Forgotten Army") in Burma. She took a four-month leave of absence from her British commitments and went on a tour of the Arakan front. On 10 May 1944 she and her accompanist, Len Edwards, performed for the men of 31 Squadron. Surviving squadron mates to this day recall her visit with great fondness.

Lynn retired from performing at the end of the war but returned to the stage in 1947. She signed with Decca Records in the United States and garnered a top-ten hit with "You Can't Be True, Dear," and in 1952 she became the first British artist to hit number one on the U.S. charts with "Auf Wiedersehn, Sweetheart." She was still active in the 1970s but cut back on public appearances in the 1980s. In 1976 she was made Dame Vera Lynn.

> *We'll meet again, don't know where, don't know when,*
> *But I know we'll meet again some sunny day.*
> *Keep smiling through just like you always do*
> *Till the blue skies drive the dark clouds far away.*

APPENDIX A

Audrey Hepburn

Many words have been used to capture the essence of film actress Audrey Hepburn: radiance, childlike fragility, simple elegance and style. Perhaps in playing the role of Eliza Doolittle in the movie *My Fair Lady* (1964) she was truly the "fairest of them all." She won a Best Actress Oscar for *Roman Holiday* (1953) and was subsequently nominated for Academy Awards for her performances in *Sabrina* (1954), *The Nun's Story* (1959), *Breakfast at Tiffany's* (1961), and *Wait until Dark* (1967). In 1990 she received the Cecil B. de Mille Award from the Hollywood Press Association for lifetime achievement.

(Photofest)

Few know, however, that at the age of ten Audrey Hepburn was living in Holland under a Nazi regime. Her family settled in the city of Arnhem, the site of one of the bloodiest battles following the D-Day invasion. During the German occupation of Arnhem, food was difficult to come by. Hepburn was sickly, and so hungry that she sometimes ate tulip bulbs to survive; as a result, she became very thin and anemic. Much of the family property was confiscated by the occupying troops, and their home was appropriated by Nazi officers.

From an early age Hepburn had studied dance, and during the occupation she continued her dance classes at the Arnhem Conservatory of Music. Her half-brother, who was a member of the Dutch Army, went into hiding to avoid capture. He was eventually apprehended, however, and sent to a German prison camp. In 1942 her uncle, Otto van Limburg Stirum, was executed in reprisal for an act of sabotage. To assist the resistance movement, Hepburn and her classmates danced in fundraising events and performed behind blacked-out windows. She often acted as a courier for the resistance and carried forged ration cards and false identity papers.

On the morning of 17 September 1944, Arnhem was one of the objectives of the Allied operation Market Garden. The goal of this operation was to drive into Germany through the back door—that is, skirt the north end of the Siegfried Line—then aim for Berlin. Before the operation could be considered a success, three bridges sixty miles to the north of Gen. Bernard Montgomery's 21st Army Group in northern Belgium had to be secured so that his army could begin their push northward. Thirty-five thousand paratroopers were dropped near the bridges at Eindhoven, Nijmegen, and Arnhem. The U.S. 82nd and 101st Airborne Divisions took the Eindhoven and Nijmegen bridges after brief combat, but the British 1st Airborne Division and the Polish Parachute Brigade ran into fierce opposition and became entrapped at Arnhem. German Panzer divisions, artillery, and ground attacks soundly defeated these units, and of nine thousand British and Polish soldiers who fought at Arnhem, only two thousand made it back to Allied lines. Because of the Dutch resistance's role in the battle, the people of Arnhem were ordered out of the city, and the Germans subsequently destroyed it. Hepburn and her mother joined the masses of people clogging the road leading out of the city. Hepburn remembered,

"It was human misery at its starkest. Masses of refugees on the move, some carrying their dead, babies born on the roadside, hundreds collapsing of hunger." It was during this time that malnutrition may have permanently damaged Hepburn's metabolism, which led to her lifelong inability to gain weight. The destruction of Arnhem became the subject of the British film *A Bridge Too Far* (1977), directed by Richard Attenborough.

On 4 May 1945 the Netherlands was liberated, and Canadian troops marched into what was left of Arnhem. Many of the townspeople had returned, among them Hepburn and her mother. Hepburn recalled, "We whooped and hollered and danced for joy. I wanted to kiss every one of them. . . . Freedom is . . . like something in the air. For me, it was hearing soldiers speaking English instead of German and smelling real tobacco smoke again from their cigarettes."

Hepburn's mother wanted her daughter to continue with her ballet lessons, and they moved to Amsterdam, which held greater promise for the talented young student. Performing in various small theater productions, she eventually won a ballet scholarship that required another move, this time to London. While training there she began to win modeling assignments from fashion photographers, and in the early 1950s she began to take acting lessons. She received her first big break when the French novelist Colette saw her and insisted that she play the lead in a forthcoming Broadway adaptation of her *Gigi.* Hepburn received such glowing critical acclaim for that performance that she was cast opposite Gregory Peck in the film *Roman Holiday,* a role for which she was awarded an Oscar for Best Actress in 1953. That same year she won a Tony Award for her performance in the Broadway play *Ondine.* She appeared in several successful films in the 1950s, married actor Mel Ferrer in 1954, and appeared with him in the films *War and Peace* (1957) and *Green Mansions* (1959).

Although she was not nominated for an Academy Award for her performance in *My Fair Lady* (1964), Hepburn will probably be most remembered for her role in that delightful musical. Alton Cook of the *New York World-Telegraph* wrote of her, "Probably no man alive has seen all the Eliza Doolittles since George Bernard Shaw put her on the stage in his 1912 *Pygmalion,* which inspired the musical. Nevertheless, I am laying bets Audrey Hepburn must be the most delightful in the long procession of Elizas. Every movie Audrey makes seems exquisitely right."

After making *My Fair Lady*, Hepburn appeared in few movies. She divorced Ferrer in 1968 and married an Italian psychiatrist, Andrea Dotti, and lived in Rome and later in Switzerland. For the rest of her life she devoted herself to charity work. She was named Special Ambassador for UNICEF and often visited the war-torn countries of Africa. Her health failed her in her later years, and she died in 1993 at the age of sixty-six.

Rin Tin Tin

During the 1920s there were an extraordinary number of animals appearing in silent movies. There was Mack Sennett's elephant Anna May, who went on to a successful career in Tarzan movies; the lions Numa and Duke; Susie the chicken; the monkey Josephine, who could play pool and golf, and a pair of acting monkeys called the Dippity-Do-Dads; Lillian Gish's cats; Tom Mix's horse Tony, William S. Hart's horse Fritz, and Rex the Wonder Horse; an alligator, a parrot, and a turtle. All appeared in more than one movie, and they could perform in some manner on cue. Some received fan mail, and they were constantly written up in movie magazines.

Dogs were the most popular of animal thespians. They came in all

(Photofest)

breeds and sizes. Audiences were enchanted by these performers, perhaps seeing in them something of their own pets. One dog, however, stood out from the others, including more recent stars such as Lassie, Benji, and Beethoven, and that canine was Rin Tin Tin.

At the peak of his career in the late 1920s, Rin Tin Tin received twelve thousand fan letters a week, earned $6,000 a month, was insured for $100,000, and had a press agent, a valet, and a chef who prepared châteaubriand with all the trimmings for the four-legged actor. He had a limo and driver, and there was always an orchestra on the set playing mood music for him while he performed. He had eighteen doubles to stand in for him when he was tired, a personal secretary to handle his schedule, a diamond-studded collar to wear, his own production unit, and a lucrative contract with Ken-L Rations, whereby his picture appeared on every box of the company's very popular dog biscuits.

Rin Tin Tin's rise from rags to riches reads much like a fairy tale. In September 1918 a group of airmen from the 136th Aero Division, which included American doughboy Cpl. Lee Duncan (1893–1960), were in France scouting out a site for a new field headquarters. They stumbled upon an abandoned German war dog station in which they found a starving female German shepherd with five new puppies. Duncan, an animal lover, convinced his commanding officer that the animals should be taken back to their hangar and safety. When the war ended he took two of the pups, a female and a male, back to the States with him. He named them Nanette and Rin Tin Tin, the names of the finger-length dolls French soldiers carried with them into battle.

Nanette died of pneumonia shortly after Duncan returned home, but Rin Tin Tin fared well and grew into a handsome, sturdy animal. Duncan noticed almost immediately how quickly the dog learned the most complex tricks. Being something of an entrepreneur, he decided to train the dog for the movies. Nicknamed Rinty, the dog was presented to movie mogul Jack L. Warner, who was so impressed with the animal that he cast him in the feature film *Where the North Begins* (1923). Rinty was tagged as a good actor by movie critics, and his public appeal was almost instantaneous.

Rinty was a natural scene stealer who could move audiences by looking hurt, worried, sad, or happy. When he laid his head in the lap of a co-star and looked up at the person with his big brown eyes, the human performer was quickly overshadowed. Rinty was a superlative stunt dog as well, often appearing in cliff-hanging scenes. During his early films he would often look off camera to Duncan for instructions. As he became seasoned, however, he learned to perform on his own and had an uncanny knack of knowing what was expected of him during his scenes. The dog possessed almost human ingenuity. He was also so professional that during a shoot he could hold a pose for thirty minutes without moving a whisker while the set was properly lit. He could work for hours, performing as if he understood the story line of the film. As audiences watched him do his stunts and appear to think out solutions, they began to perceive him as more human than canine. Movie magazines treated him as if he were in fact human and during so-called interviews would concoct answers for him to give to their rather inane questions.

Over the next nine years Rinty appeared in twenty-four movies and became Warner Brothers' top box-office draw. He came to be known as "the mortgage lifter" because his movies often bailed the studio out of financial difficulties and kept it solvent. He also helped the career of a young screenwriter, Darryl Francis Zanuck, who wrote a number of Rinty's scripts under the name Gregory Rogers. Zanuck would later become the head of 20th Century Fox Studios.

Eventually, as talkies took over the industry, less attention was paid to movie animals, especially dogs. Critics began to grow tired of seeing wonder dogs in movies and longed for just plain old dogs. Fan magazines carried fewer and fewer stories and photo spreads on these unique thespians. Rinty was still a star when the craze began to fade, and when Warner Brothers movie stars including the animals were introduced to the public in a 1929 sound film *Show of Shows,* Rinty led the way. His fans were not disappointed, since his bark was loud and sharp, and he recorded well. He had made the transition with ease, but his popularity began to fade, and fewer movie opportunities came his way. The studio released him in 1930. He made a couple of low-budget serial films before retiring a year later.

During the latter days of his career Rinty had mated with another movie shepherd named Nanette, and they had four male puppies. The event made world headlines. One of the puppies enjoyed a short film career. Rin Tin Tin, Jr., made a number of serials in the 1930s for Mascot Studios.

On 10 August 1932, at the age of fourteen, Rinty collapsed while playing with Duncan on the lawn in front of Duncan's home. As Duncan cradled him in his arms, devastated by the sudden turn of events, a neighbor from across the street came running to see what had happened. The lady, who loved the animal as much as Duncan did, took the dog in her embrace and sobbed as she held him. So it was that Rin Tin Tin died in the arms of famed actress Jean Harlow.

Bibliography

Alpert, Hollis. *Burton.* New York: G. P. Putnam's Sons, 1986.

Attenborough, R. *In Search of Ghandi.* London: Bodley Head, 1982.

Aumont, Jean-Pierre. *Sun and Shadow.* New York: W. W. Norton and Co., 1977.

Bogarde, Dirk. *Cleared for Take-off.* London: Viking, 1995.

———. *Snakes and Ladders.* New York: Holt, Rinehart, and Winston, 1979.

Bragg, Melvyn. *Richard Burton: A Life.* New York: Warner, 1988.

Caine, Michael. *Raising Caine.* New Jersey: Prentice-Hall, 1982.

———. *What's It All About: An Autobiography.* New York: Turtle Bay/Random House, 1992.

Callan, Michael Feeny. *Anthony Hopkins: An Unauthorized Biography.* New York: Scribner's/Maxwell Macmillan International, 1994.

———. *Sean Connery: His Life and Films.* Philadelphia: Stein and Day, 1983.

Callow, Simon. *Charles Laughton: A Difficult Actor.* London: Methuen, 1987.

Cole, Stephen. *Noel Coward: A Biography.* Westport, Conn.: Greenwood, 1993.

Colman, Juliet Benita. *Ronald Colman.* New York: Morrow, 1975.

Current Biography Yearbook. New York: H. W. Wilson, 1940–98.

Donovan, Paul. *Roger Moore.* Philadelphia: W. H. Allen/Comet, 1983.

Druxman, Michael. *Basil Rathbone: His Life in Films.* South Brunswick, N.J.: A. S. Barnes and Co., 1975.

Dundy, Elaine. *Finch Bloody Finch: A Life of Peter Finch.* New York: Holt, Rinehart, and Winston, 1980.

Elliott, Susan, with Barry Turner. *Denholm Elliott: A Quest for Love.* London: Headline, 1994.

Falk, Quentin. *Anthony Hopkins: The Authorized Biography.* New York: Interlink, 1994.

Faulkner, Trader. *Peter Finch: A Biography.* London: Angus and Robertson, 1979.

Ferris, Paul. *Richard Burton.* New York: Coward, McGann, and Geoghagen, 1981.

Finch, Yolande. *Finchy.* New York: Wyndham, 1981.

Frank, Sam. *Ronald Colman: A Bio-Bibliography.* Westport, Conn.: Greenwood, 1997.

Freedman, Michael. *Peter O'Toole.* Philadelphia: W. H. Allen, 1984.

———. *Sean Connery: A Biography.* London: Orion, 1994.

Gallagher, Elaine. *Candidly Caine.* London: Robeson, 1991.

Granger, Stewart. *Sparks Fly Upward.* New York: G. P. Putnam's Sons, 1981.

Guinness, Alec. *Blessings in Disguise.* New York: Alfred A. Knopf, 1980.

Hardwicke, Cedric. *Let's Pretend.* London: Grayson and Grayson, 1932.

Harrison, Rex. *A Damned Serious Business: My Life in Comedy.* New York: Bantam, 1991.

———. *Rex: An Autobiography.* New York: Morrow, 1975.

Hawkins, Jack. *Anything but a Quiet Life.* New York: Stein and Day, 1974.

Higham, Charles. *Charles Laughton: An Intimate Biography.* New York: Doubleday and Co., 1976.

Hilton, James. *Lost Horizon.* New York: Simon and Schuster, 1933.

Holden, Anthony. *Laurence Olivier: A Biography.* New York: Collier, 1990.

Howard, Leslie. *A Quite Remarkable Father.* New York: Harcourt Brace and Co., 1959.

Howard, Ronald. *In Search of My Father.* New York: St. Martin's, 1981.

Hunter, Alan. *Alec Guinness on Screen.* Edinburgh: Polygon, 1982.

Judge, Philip. *Michael Caine.* New York: Hippocrene, 1985.

Junor, Penny. *Burton: The Man behind the Myth.* London: Sidgewick and Jackson, 1985.

Katz, Ephraim. *The Film Encyclopedia,* 3d ed. New York: Harper Perennial, 1998.

Knight, Vivienne. *Trevor Howard: A Gentleman and a Player.* New York: Beaufort, 1986.

Lamparski, Richard. *What Ever Became of . . . ?* New York: Crown, 1967.

Larkin, Robert. *Chips: The Life and Films of Chips Rafferty.* New York: Macmillan, 1986.

Lee, Christopher. *Tall, Dark, and Gruesome.* London: Victor Gollancz/Wellington House, 1997.

Lynn, Vera. *Vocal Refrain.* London: W. H. Allen, 1975.

Macnee, Patrick, and Marie Cameron. *Blind in One Ear.* San Francisco: Mercury House, 1989.

Macnee, Patrick, with Dave Rogers. *The Avengers and Me.* New York: TV Books, 1997.

Maltin, Leonard. *Leonard Maltin's Movie Encyclopedia.* New York: Penguin, 1995.

———. *2000 Movie and Video Guide.* New York: Penguin, 2000.

McFarlane, Brian. *An Autobiography of British Cinema.* London: Random House, 1988.

Milland, Ray. *Wide-Eyed in Babylon.* London: Bodley Head, 1979.

Mills, John. *Up in the Clouds, Gentlemen Please.* Boston: Ticknor and Fields, 1981.

Morley, Sheridan. *Tales from the Hollywood Raj: The British, the Movies, and Tinseltown.* New York: Viking, 1983.

Moseley, Roy. *Roger Moore: A Biography.* London: New English Library, 1985.

Moseley, Roy, and Phillip Masheter. *Rex Harrison: A Biography.* New York: St. Martin's, 1987.

Munn, Michael. *Stars at War.* London: Robeson, 1995.

———. *Trevor Howard: The Man and His Films.* London: Scarborough House, 1990.

Nalty, Bernard C. *The Vietnam War: The History of America's Conflict in Southeast Asia.* New York: Salamander, 1996.

Niven, David. *The Moon's a Balloon.* New York: Dell, 1972.

Olivier, Laurence. *Laurence Olivier: Confessions of an Actor.* New York: Simon and Schuster, 1992.

O'Toole, Peter. *Loitering with Intent.* New York: Hyperion, 1992.

Passingham, Kim. *Sean Connery: A Biography.* New York: St. Martin's, 1983.

"Personality & War Film—Lieutenant Kenneth More." *After the Battle* 17 (1977).

"Personality & War Film—Lieutenant Richard Todd." *After the Battle* 5 (1974): 40–42.

"Personality & War Film—Major Anthony Quayle." *After the Battle* 15 (1977): 36–38.

Pitts, Michael. *Horror Film Stars.* Jefferson, N.C.: McFarland and Co., 1991.

Pope, Stephen, and Elizabeth-Anne Wheal. *The Dictionary of the First World War.* New York: St. Martin's, 1995.

Rathbone, Basil. *In and out of Character.* New York: Doubleday and Co., 1962.

Rigby, Jonathan. *Christopher Lee: The Authorized Screen History.* London: Reynolds and Hearn, 2001.

Ross, Lillian, and Helen Ross. *The Player: Profile of an Art.* New York: Simon and Schuster, 1962.

Smith, R. Dixon. *Ronald Colman: Gentleman of the Cinema.* Jefferson, N.C.: McFarland and Co., 1991.

Spoto, Donald. *Laurence Olivier: A Biography.* New York: Harper Collins, 1992.

Stevenson, Tyrone. *Richard Burton: A Biography.* Westport, Conn.: Greenwood, 1992.

Tanitch, Robert. *John Mills.* London: Collins and Brown, 1993.

Taylor, John Russell. *Alec Guinness.* Boston: Little, Brown and Co., 1984.

Thomas, Terry. *Filling the Gap.* London: Max Parrish and Co., 1959.

Thomas, Tony. *Ustinov in Focus.* New York: A. S. Barnes and Co., 1971.

Todd, Richard. *Caught in the Act.* London: Century Hutchinson, 1987.

Unterburger, Amy L. *International Dictionary of Films and Film Makers.* Vol. 3, *Actors and Actresses.* New York: St. James, 1997.

Ustinov, Peter. *Dear Me.* London: William Heinemann, 1977.

———. *Ustinov Still at Large.* Amherst, N.Y.: Prometheus, 1995.

The Variety Insider: Editors of Variety. New York: Berkley, 1999.

Vermilye, Jerry. *Audrey Hepburn: Her Life and Career.* Secaucus, N.J.: Carol, 1998.

Wapshott, Nicholas. *Peter O'Toole.* London: New English Library, 1983.

———. *Rex Harrison.* London: Chatto and Windus, 1991.

Williams, Geoffrey. *Peter Ustinov.* London: Peter Owen, 1958.

Wood, Ean. *The Josephine Baker Story.* London: Sanctuary, 2000.

Yule, Andrew. *Sean Connery: From 007 to Hollywood Icon.* New York: Donald Fine, 1992.

Index

About the Authors

James E. Wise, Jr., became a naval aviator in 1953 following graduation from Northwestern University. He served as an intelligence officer aboard USS *America* (CVA-66) and later as the commanding officer of various naval intelligence units.

Since his retirement from the Navy in 1975 as a captain, Wise has held several senior executive posts in private sector companies. In addition to *Stars in Blue: Movie Actors in America's Sea Services, Stars in the Corps: Movie Actors in the United States Marines,* and *Stars in Khaki: Movie Actors in the Army and the Air Services,* he is the co-author with Otto Giese of *Shooting the War: The Memoir and Photographs of a U-Boat Officer in World War II.* He is also the author of many articles published in naval and maritime journals. He lives in Alexandria, Virginia.

Scott Baron served for two years as an enlisted man in the U.S. Army during the Vietnam War. Following his military service, he graduated cum laude from California State University–Northridge with a degree in constitutional law and worked for a decade in law enforcement prior to teaching at Evergreen Criminal Justice Center (police academy) and Cabrillo Community College in Aptos, California.

He is the author of *They Also Served: Military Biographies of Uncommon Americans* and *Nevada Law Enforcement Cloth Insignia* (two volumes). He is also a contributing writer for *Stars and Stripes,* both the newspaper and the Web site, and has written articles on military history and crime prevention for various publications. He currently teaches eighth grade American history at Washington Middle School in Salinas, California. Mr. Baron lives in Watsonville with his wife and two sons.

The Naval Institute Press is the book-publishing arm of the U.S. Naval Institute, a private, nonprofit, membership society for sea service professionals and others who share an interest in naval and maritime affairs. Established in 1873 at the U.S. Naval Academy in Annapolis, Maryland, where its offices remain today, the Naval Institute has members worldwide.

Members of the Naval Institute support the education programs of the society and receive the influential monthly magazine *Proceedings* and discounts on fine nautical prints and on ship and aircraft photos. They also have access to the transcripts of the Institute's Oral History Program and get discounted admission to any of the Institute-sponsored seminars offered around the country.

The Naval Institute also publishes *Naval History* magazine. This colorful bimonthly is filled with entertaining and thought-provoking articles, first-person reminiscences, and dramatic art and photography. Members receive a discount on *Naval History* subscriptions.

The Naval Institute's book-publishing program, begun in 1898 with basic guides to naval practices, has broadened its scope to include books of more general interest. Now the Naval Institute Press publishes about one hundred titles each year, ranging from how-to books on boating and navigation to battle histories, biographies, ship and aircraft guides, and novels. Institute members receive significant discounts on the Press's more than eight hundred books in print.

Full-time students are eligible for special half-price membership rates. Life memberships are also available.

For a free catalog describing Naval Institute Press books currently available, and for further information about subscribing to *Naval History* magazine or about joining the U.S. Naval Institute, please write to:

Membership Department
U.S. Naval Institute
291 Wood Road
Annapolis, MD 21402-5034
Telephone: (800) 233-8764
Fax: (410) 269-7940
Web address: www.navalinstitute.org